Computerized Literature Searching

Also of Interest

Introduction to Library Research in Education, Jamie Wright Coniglio

Toward Effective Strategic Analysis: New Applications of Information Technology, Albert Clarkson

Introduction to Library Research in Women's Studies, Susan E. Searing

Secure Communications and Asymmetric Cryptosystems, edited by Gustavus J. Simmons

Doing Library Research: An Introduction for Community College Students, Robert K. Baker

†*Introduction to Library Research in French Literature,* Robert K. Baker

Introduction to Library Research in German Studies, Larry L. Richardson

Information Services: Economics, Management, and Technology, edited by Robert M. Mason and John E. Creps

†*The Library of Congress,* Second Edition, Charles A. Goodrum and Helen W. Dalrymple

†Available in hardcover and paperback.

Westview Special Studies in
Information Science and Management

Computerized Literature Searching: Research Strategies and Databases

Charles L. Gilreath

The computer terminal is well on its way to being as commonplace as the telephone, and its usefulness to the scholar and scientist is so great that already computer screens and disks are seen frequently in academic offices. The value of computers in research is well established, with vast amounts of data being processed daily by all sizes of computers. Computers also have had dramatic effects on the researcher's literature-searching options: Scientists and scholars can now query enormous databases containing tens of millions of citations to published literature and can extract bibliographies tailored to their specific questions. The power and flexibility afforded the user of information by these literature-searching systems ease the burden of library work, but in order to use the systems effectively, it is necessary to understand both their capabilities and their limitations.

Mr. Gilreath describes the principles underlying online bibliographic systems, the databases available, and the factors a researcher must consider in using them. He explores in some depth the relationship of the structure and terminology of publications in various fields to the literature-searching process and provides detailed guidelines for research in the life, health, agricultural, and social sciences, chemistry, physics, mathematics, geology, meteorology, engineering, education, psychology, business, law, current affairs, and the humanities. A glossary of literature-searching terms is included.

Charles L. Gilreath is head of the Automated Information Retrieval Service for Texas A&M University Library. He is the author of *CAIN Online User's Guide* (1976), *AGRICOLA User's Guide* (1979), and "Computerized Data Bases for Bibliographic Research" in Richard Blanchard's *Guide to Sources for Agricultural and Biological Research* (1981).

Computerized Literature Searching: Research Strategies and Databases

Charles L. Gilreath

Routledge
Taylor & Francis Group
LONDON AND NEW YORK

First published 1984 by Westview Press, Inc.

Published 2018 by Routledge
52 Vanderbilt Avenue, New York, NY 10017
2 Park Square, Milton Park, Abingdon, Oxon OX14 4RN

Routledge is an imprint of the Taylor & Francis Group, an informa business

Library of Congress Cataloging in Publication Data
Gilreath, Charles L.
Computerized literature searching.
(Westview special studies in information science and management)
Includes index.
1. Online bibliographic searching. 2. Machine-readable bibliographic data. 3. Information retrieval. 4. Research—Methodology—Data processing. I. Title. II. Series.
Z699.G56 1984 025.5'24 83-23319
ISBN 13: 978-0-367-01968-6(hbk)

Contents

List of Figures ix
Acknowledgments xi
Introduction xiii

1 The Basics of Computer Literature Search Systems 1

Organizing Information 6
Printed Indexes 8
Computer Retrieval Systems 13
Constraints on Computer Systems 14

2 The Researcher–Search Analyst Partnership 17

3 Agricultural and Life Sciences 23

Characteristics and Terminology 23
Profiling Assistance 27
Databases 38

4 Social Sciences and Education 52

Characteristics and Terminology 52
Profiling Assistance 55
Databases 63

5 Physical Sciences and Engineering 81

Characteristics and Terminology 81
Profiling Assistance 88
Databases 95

6 Business Literature ... 119

Characteristics and Terminology ... 119
Profiling Assistance ... 122
Databases ... 129

7 Humanities, the Arts, and Architecture ... 140

Characteristics and Terminology ... 140
Profiling Assistance ... 145
Databases ... 148
Notes ... 152

8 Legal Research ... 153

Characteristics and Terminology ... 153
Profiling Assistance ... 159
Databases ... 161

Glossary ... 165
Index ... 170

Figures

1-1 Hypothetical search sequence 4

1-2 Production and transmission of information 7

1-3 KWIC and KWOC indexes 10

1-4 Coordinate indexing system using cards 11

1-5 Steps in the use of a coordinate index 12

1-6 Permuted title word index from *Social Sciences Citation Index* 13

2-1 Strategy for search on creativity 19

3-1 *MeSH* tree structure 34

3-2 AGRICOLA and BIOSIS code schemes 37

3-3 BIOSIS citation illustrating the weighting of terms in the Concept Code field 38

4-1 Entry from *Thesaurus of ERIC Descriptors* 56

4-2 Entry from *Political Science Thesaurus* categorized display 58

5-1 Partial strategy for retrieving information on properties of gallium and arsenic compounds 83

5-2 Alternative strategies for a search on computer techniques for extraction of square roots 87

5-3 Citation from *Chemical Abstracts,* volume 87 90

5-4 Entry from the *Energy Data Base Subject Thesaurus* 92

6-1 Entry from cited reference section of *Social Sciences Citation Index* 124

6-2 Standard Industrial Classification code numbers 127

6-3 Selection from ABI/INFORM classification scheme ... 128

8-1 Comparison of search results between a full text file and indexing/abstracting service files 158

Acknowledgments

First, I would like to express my gratitude to Mr. Frederick Praeger, who sparked the idea of the book during a 1981 visit to Texas A&M to deliver a lecture on the future of scholarly publishing. At the time he mused that he might be delivering the funeral oration for that endeavor. I prefer to think that with men of his enthusiasm around, we may see, rather than the death of scholarly publishing, an intelligent transfiguration.

My thanks go also to a talented student assistant, Sohail Bokhari, for his invaluable assistance with the illustrations.

Finally, my thanks to my wife, Ann, who endured the initial writing and then proofread the results. The mistakes that remain I claim for myself.

C.L.G.

Introduction

To assert that the computer has profoundly affected scholarship is to understate the case. Indeed, computer technology has opened avenues of research only dreamed of fifty years ago and but dimly understood even twenty years ago. The computer's impact on scholarly communication and library research is of more recent origin, yet in the past decade computer systems have begun to reshape at all levels the process of recording, transmitting, storing, and retrieving information.

As with many advances, the new technology forces the user to examine old methods, to think critically about those processes and techniques so long taken for granted. Such is the case with the computer systems that have been developed to assist in literature searching. The mechanics of computerized information retrieval make it relatively easy to pull some relevant citations from databases such as Sociological Abstracts or Zoological Record, but retrieving information in the most effective manner requires a thorough understanding of how information is organized. In the space of a single volume one cannot, of course, cover comprehensively the subtle differences in dozens of research fields. It is the goal of this work, rather, to alert the user of computerized library research services to potential problem areas and to cause him or her to ask the right questions in order to achieve the best results.

The user for whom this work is principally intended is the scientist or advanced student who is generally familiar with research in a given field but who may not know how to approach the development of search strategies for using computer literature-searching systems. Librarians and information specialists who have been called upon to conduct literature searches in fields unfamiliar to them will, one hopes, also find aid and comfort in these pages. The focus throughout has been on the subject matter and the structure of information in broad fields rather than on the selection or operation of specific retrieval systems, for which information abounds elsewhere.

The book is organized into eight sections: two chapters giving a general overview of computer library research systems and their capabilities and six others discussing research strategies for broad areas of research. Each discipline-oriented chapter is divided into three parts: a discussion of the general characteristics and the terminology peculiar to that field, a description of profiling aids that might be employed in constructing a search strategy, and a selective list of commonly available databases for that field.

1
The Basics of Computer Literature Search Systems

In 1946, when the 19,000 tubes of the ENIAC computer began to glow dimly at the University of Pennsylvania, a new era of information processing was born. Originally conceived as high-speed calculating machines to help scientists solve complex equations, the generations of computers descending from ENIAC have evolved into powerful general purpose logic machines capable of manipulating enormous banks of data. The pervasiveness of this technology in society is nearly impossible to fathom. Today computers touch us in almost every aspect of our lives, from calculating and printing electric utility bills to controlling the flow of traffic on city streets, from recording vital statistics of newborns to editing the text of newspaper obituary columns. Computer technology has forced us to develop new skills virtually undreamed of by our great-grandparents and to do traditional jobs in radically different ways. Like the rest of the world, libraries have been significantly affected by the computer revolution, some having joined eagerly and others finding themselves swept along by the succeeding waves of technological change.

Generally the evolution of automation in research libraries has been led by those activities most heavily utilizing clerical time, that is, the purchasing, cataloging, and circulation of books and other library materials. Automated circulation systems, usually run on in-house or at least locally owned computers, have relieved both library staff and patrons of much of the drudgery required for maintaining records of book circulations. Large national or regional computer systems, such as those developed and operated by OCLC, Inc., the Research Libraries Group, and the Washington Library Network, have been highly successful in speeding the cataloging process for their member libraries. Using one of these shared cataloging systems, a person sitting at a computer terminal in Texas can locate cataloging copy for a book, enter whatever changes are desired to make that record meet local library standards, order a set of cataloging cards, and share with member libraries in Kentucky or Rhode Island the fact that that item is now available for loan in Texas—all in a fraction of the time it used to take to type a set of cards to file in the local catalog.

Used in their traditional way, circulation and cataloging systems are essentially behind-the-scenes operations that affect only minimally the way people use libraries. New developments in the nature of these record-keeping systems, however, will soon have a dramatic impact on how information can be retrieved from libraries. In the next few years it will be possible for patrons of many libraries to go to a terminal—perhaps even in their homes or offices—and dial up the library's computer. Once connected, they can query the system for books on any subject. Having identified the ones they want, they can determine whether those books are available for checkout. In some instances, the library users may even be able to request that the books be held for them until they can get to the library to charge them out.

Perhaps more dramatic in its potential impact on library research methods has been the development of computer systems to search indexes, abstracting services, directories, and other traditional reference tools. Over the past fifteen years the publishers of indexing and abstracting services have invested heavily in automation. Entries for such services are today typically prepared and edited in machine-readable form. A computer tape is prepared, which is subsequently used to drive typesetting equipment or to photocompose directly camera-ready pages for printing. These edited computer tapes have become an increasingly valuable resource as the basis of large machine-readable databases. The mere existence of a machine-readable file does not, of course, have much impact on the retrieval of information by individuals conducting research. Slow and inefficient computer programs to search machine-readable files are no better—and sometimes worse—than manual search techniques.

The mid-1960s, however, saw the development of computer systems that made possible the fast retrieval and manipulation of bibliographic information. These systems allowed users to query bibliographic databases for words and phrases that might appear in the citations and, in a conversational mode, to modify the results of the search. Thus it became possible for researchers to go to one of these systems, pose questions and, based on the results of the queries, adjust the answers so that they got out of the system a list of references tailored to their information needs. Because online systems such as these require such enormous storage capacity, they are too expensive for most libraries to consider operating locally, but through subscription to any of a number of computer services that provide dial-up access to timeshared computing centers, many libraries can gain access to literally millions of machine-readable records in order to provide interactive searching of vast stores of information.

Two of the earliest and most successful computer retrieval systems are System Development Corporation's (SDC) ORBIT and Lockheed (now DIALOG) Information Service's DIALOG. Both of these retrieval packages were developed in the late 1960s under government contract. SDC developed its ORBIT system to make the National Library of Medicine's MEDLARS (Medical Literature Automated Retrieval System) searchable in a conversational mode, while Lockheed developed the prototype of its DIALOG system as the RECON (Remote Console) system for NASA. The years since these early systems began operation have seen the development of many other retrieval systems throughout the world. By 1982 it was estimated that there were actually dozens of retrieval systems in operation providing online access to tens of millions of bibliographic and factual records.

In operation each retrieval system may look quite different to the uninitiated observer, but whatever system is used—DIALOG's, SDC's or another system from any of the burgeoning number of information services now in the field—the basic organization and operation is the same. Figure 1-1 (a hypothetical search sequence) illustrates many of these features.

In this example the computer system prompts the user each time it is ready to accept additional commands through the cues for each statement and the word "USER." Its own responses

```
*STATEMENT #1

USER:  FIND AUTOMOBILES OR CARS

PROG:  (1500)

*STATEMENT #2

USER:  FIND SALES

PROG:  (10,647)

*STATEMENT #3

USER:  FIND FORECAST$ OR PROJECT$ OR PREDICT$

PROG:  (8,101)

*STATEMENT #4

USER:  MATCH 1 AND 2 AND 3

PROG:  (18)

*STATEMENT #5

USER:  LIMIT 4 TO YR=1981

PROG:  (4)

*STATEMENT #6

USER:  PRINT 2 TITLES SS#5

PROG:

1

TI - GM PREDICTS SALES UPTURN FOR SUMMER OF 1982.

2

TI - DOMESTIC AUTOMOBILE SALES PROJECTIONS, 1981-82.
```

Figure 1-1. Hypothetical search sequence

are labelled "PROG." After each system cue, the user enters a part of the search strategy, in this instance using the commands "FIND," "MATCH," "LIMIT," and "PRINT." After each instruction from the user, the system responds with a number, indicating how many references in the database meet the requirements of that statement. Thus, the first response from the system shows that there are 1,500 references in which either "automobiles" or "cars" appears in the parts of the reference searched by the computer. The dollar signs in statement 3 are truncation symbols, signaling the system that all words beginning with the preceding characters are acceptable; thus words with many possible forms can be searched with minimal keying. The vast numbers of citations retrieved can be matched against each other in order to narrow search results to that much smaller number meeting the various aspects of the search logic. Usually in such a match the numbers drop dramatically, as in the results of statement 4, which represents those items in the hypothetical database which should be on automobile sales forecasts.

Retrieval systems, by one means or another, usually allow users to manipulate search results in other ways as well, as illustrated by statement 5, in which the eighteen citations in the previous statement are limited to those items published in 1981. Once narrowed sufficiently, the results are sampled by requesting a printout of selected titles. If the sample is acceptable, the user can choose to have a full bibliography of the results printed out either immediately at the terminal while it is still connected to the system or later at the computer facility and sent through the mail.

The flexibility that these systems provide represents a quantum leap for the researcher who must use bibliographic reference tools. Some of the differences between manual and online searches of literature are obvious; after all, with one, printed volumes are consulted and with the other, a computer terminal is employed. Other aspects of this new technology for literature searching are more subtle, but their impact on the way one carries out a library research project is significant. The chapters that follow will provide more detailed discussions of online research methods in specific disciplines, but it will be useful here to look briefly at the major aspects of both manual and computerized versions of indexing and abstracting services.

Organizing Information

Before turning to the more specific problem of how information retrieval systems are put together, one needs to consider for a moment the more general issue of information organization. Figure 1-2 represents one conception of how information is produced and subsequently organized for retrieval. At one extreme is the author who has discovered something about reality and, wishing to communicate with others, writes up the discovery as an article and submits it for publication. If the article is accepted, it will be edited and eventually published and distributed to the subscribers of the journal. A recipient of that journal may then read the article and make use of its contents right away or, if the information is not needed immediately, may file the journal away for future reference. A researcher with an unusually keen memory may be able to come back directly to that article in the future but will more likely have to rely on some secondary tool as a memory aid. These secondary tools can take many forms, ranging from a simple card file on the researcher's desk to the elaborate multivolume abstracting and indexing services such as *Chemical Abstracts* or *Zoological Record.*

The primary point to be remembered from this illustration is that communication between authors and readers is highly complex. At each stage in the flow of information from the author or producer of the information to the library researcher or user of information there are several opportunities for the original message to become garbled. As one progresses along the continuum from author to reader, the further away from the author's manuscript one proceeds the fewer become the methods of retrieving information. For example, a journal editor may have to edit a manuscript severely in order to make it fit space requirements, and most certainly an indexing or abstracting service is going to use only a skeletal version of the original article to point the reader back to the source. The fewer access points a reader has for retrieving a reference, of course, the greater are the chances of missing relevant citations in a search

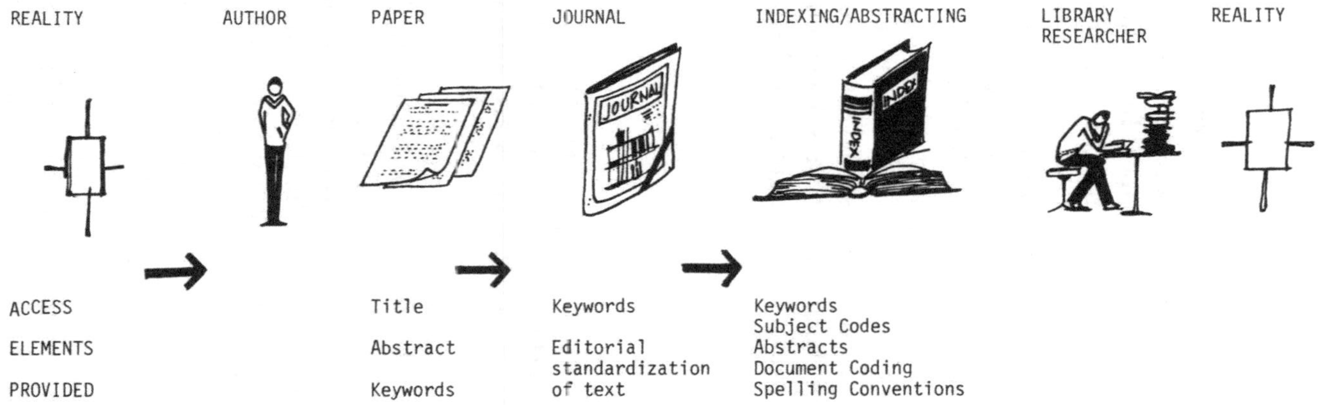

Figure 1-2. Production and transmission of information.

of the literature. The bottom portion of Figure 1-2 shows the types of access commonly provided at each stage of the information flow.

The author's own title for an article can provide many access points, provided that care is given in selecting terminology that accurately reflects the content of the paper. Depending on the journal for which the article is intended, the author may also provide a brief abstract and/or a list of keywords that may affect subsequent retrieval of articles via indexes. Finally, indexers and abstracters create document surrogates, that is, bibliographic citations that try to represent in a very brief form the most significant aspects of the original publication. Indexing citations may include the addition of keywords from a controlled list of such terms, specially prepared abstracts, and/or various other codes identifying aspects of the article such as subject, publication type (review, theoretical paper, etc.), language, and so forth.

Printed Indexes

Hierarchical Indexes

Manual literature-searching techniques rely on the structure of printed retrieval tools. Printed indexes take many forms, but all are linear devices, that is, all references are arranged in a locked sequence on the printed page. Most printed indexes are hierarchical, presenting citations in a logically arranged series of subject headings and related topical subdivisions. Users of such a work look under those headings that appear most aptly to describe the area of investigation. Having located the appropriate heading, they then read through the titles appearing under that heading to identify the ones they are interested in using for their research. Hierarchical indexes are particularly good in providing access to large volumes of literature under a carefully controlled set of categories, thereby freeing the user from having to search large numbers of individual, and sometimes idiosyncratic, terms to locate desirable references. In most instances, however, such indexes are slow to reflect changes in terminology. When new research areas emerge, some substantial period of time is usually required before new entries are introduced into the list of subject headings of printed hierarchical indexes; so the user working on a new area of specialization has to seek information under headings not quite on target for the research topic.

KWIC and KWOC Indexes

In order to overcome the shortcomings of hierarchical indexes, other approaches to indexing have been developed. KWIC (keyword-in-context) and KWOC (keyword-out-of-context) indexes provide subject access via computerized rotations of keywords and/or title words. This approach, as shown in Figure 1-3, enables the reader to search for articles that contain specific words or phrases in the title or in strings of index terms. The KWIC index also displays terms in such a way that the user can easily check the context in which the desired term appears.

Coordinate Indexes

A third type of indexing scheme, adaptable for both card files and printed retrieval aids, is the coordinate index. It is the indexing principle, as well, upon which computer literature-searching systems are based. An index based on coordinate principles first identifies each bibliographic entry by means of some unique number or letter-number tag, as shown in Figure 1-4. Indexes are built for each significant word by listing together document numbers for every item containing that word. These document number lists that constitute the index's access points are then filed or printed in alphabetic or numeric sequence. When users desire to conduct a literature search, they then consult those portions of the index containing the terms in which they are interested. By comparing item numbers they are then led back to those items in the sequential list that are likely to be of interest. Figure 1-5 illustrates the steps an engineer would go through to find articles on fatigue in prestressed concrete beams. The first step would be to look up the term "fatigue" in the index and copy down the item numbers for the references listed under that heading. Then numbers in that list must be compared with the numbers posted to the heading "prestressed concrete." Those numbers that match then go onto a second list representing those articles in the index dealing with fatigue

HANDBOOK OF	ECONOMIC STATISTICS, 1978.	20383
ONVERSION TECHNOLOGY.	ECONOMIC SYSTEM ANALYSIS OF COAL PRE	19500
ONAL CONFERENCE ON THE	ECONOMIC USE OF ELECTRIC ROAD VEHICL	17438
O ILLUSTRATING CURRENT	ECONOMIC USES OF RENEWABLE BIOMASS E	17549
O ILLUSTRATING CURRENT	ECONOMIC USES OF RENEWABLE BIOMASS E	18735
XECUTIVE CONFERENCE ON	ECONOMIC VIABILITY OF THE NUCLEAR IN	18476
ECHNIQUES: ASSOCIATED	ECONOMIC, ENVIRONMENTAL, LEGAL AND S	16883
LICY AND FORECASTING:	ECONOMIC, FINANCIAL, AND TECHNOLOGIC	19225
ERICAN COAL INDUSTRY:	ECONOMIC, POLITICAL, AND ENVIRONMENT	16649
N COAL EFFICIENTLY AND	ECONOMICALLY, AND MEET AIR POLLUTION	18177
FUTURES MARKETS. THE	ECONOMICS AND REGULATION OF PETROLEU	16716
NT PROGRAM, VOLUME V:	ECONOMICS AND SYSTEMS ANALYSIS. NUC	16948
ENERGY OPTIONS: REAL	ECONOMICS AND THE SOLAR-HYDROGEN SYS	17739
TION IN BUILDINGS: AN	ECONOMICS GUIDEBOOK FOR INVESTMENT D	20504
THE	ECONOMICS OF AMERICA'S ENERGY FUTURE	19679

a. KWIC (keyword-in-context) index from Energy Bibliography and Index, Vol. 5, (Houston: Gulf Publishing Co.), 1982.

SOCIAL ECOLOGY SOCIAL PSYCHOLOGY

KEYWORD	REFERENCE TITLE	AUTHOR	YEAR	VOL	JOUR	PAGE
PEACE	PSYCH WAR & PEACE	F ALEXANDER	1940	46	801	504
	SOCIAL PSYCH & WAR & PEACE	R STAGNER	1954	2	845	88
PEOPLE	PSYCH PEOPLE		1941	7	839	57
	PSYCH OF PEOPLE & GER		1947	13	839	22
PERCEPTION	SOCIAL PERCEPTION CORRELATE SOCIAL ADJUSTMENT	D GLASER	1957	20	874	156
	INDIV DIFF SOCIAL PERCEPTION	DN JACKSON, ETAL	1963	2	882	1
	VARIAT ADOLES PERCEP FAMILY POWER	CE BOWERMAN	1964	29	802	551
	ORIGIN PAWN VARIABLE PERSON PERCEPT	R DECHARMS	1965	28	874	241
	VERBAL & VISUAL INFO PERCEPTION	PB WARR, ETAL	1966	5	882	118
	EXPECTANCY & COMMUNICA PERCEPTION	PB WARR, ETAL	1966	5	882	244
	SELF PERCEPTION THESES & METHODOLOG	J JOHNSTON	1968	3	884	113
	PHYSICAL SOCIAL & PERSONAL PERCEPT CROWDING	D STOKOLS, ETAL	1973	5	867	87
PERCEPTIONS	SELF PERCEPTIONS & DESCRIPTIONS	RM LUNDY	1956	19	874	272

b. KWOC (keyword-out-of-context) index from Combined Retrospective Index to Journals in Sociology, 1895-1974, (Washington, D.C.: Carrollton Press), 1978.

Figure 1-3. KWIC and KWOC indexes.

in prestressed concrete structures generally. The search can be narrowed to only those items dealing specifically with beams, by turning to the item number list for the heading "beams," comparing numbers, and generating a final list of tags for those references that should be most relevant to the engineer's needs. The final step is to turn to the sequential listing of bibliographic entries, look up the items already identified, and select specific items to read.

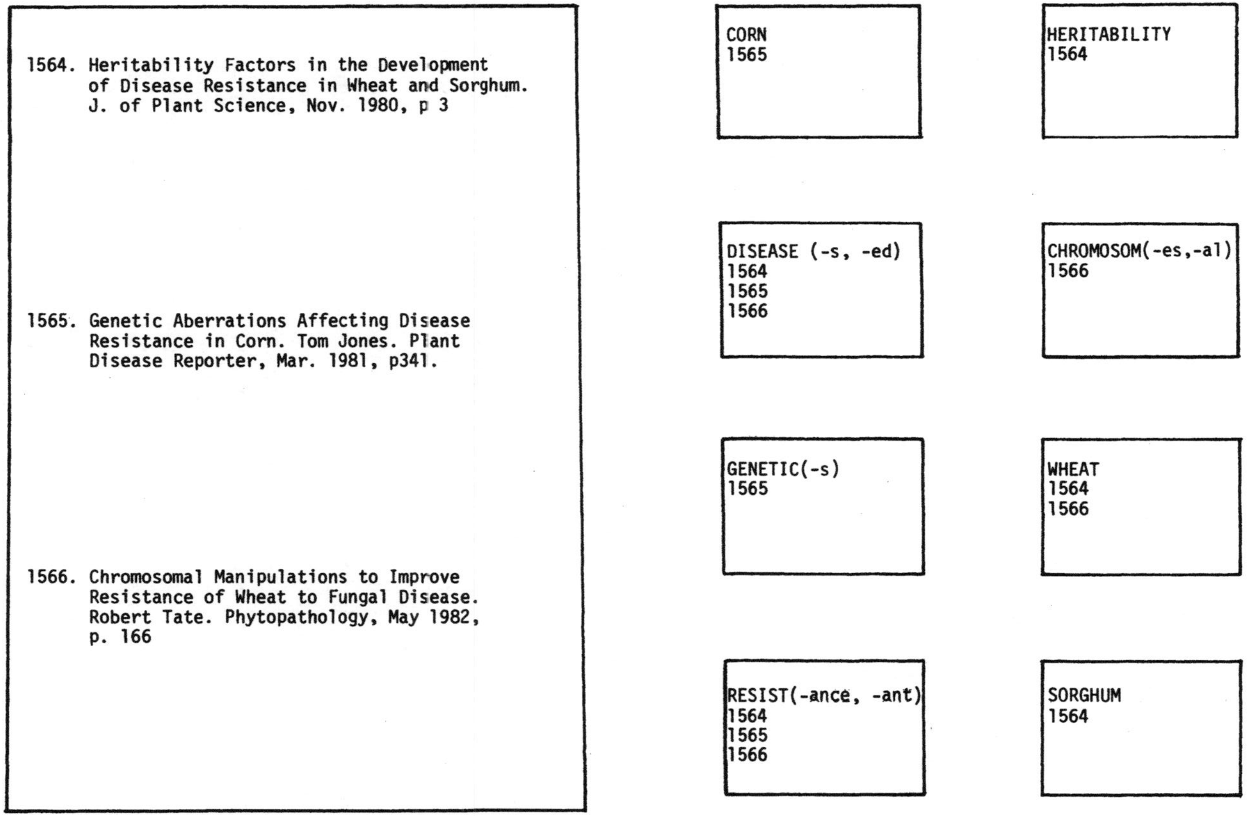

Figure 1-4. Coordinate indexing system using cards.

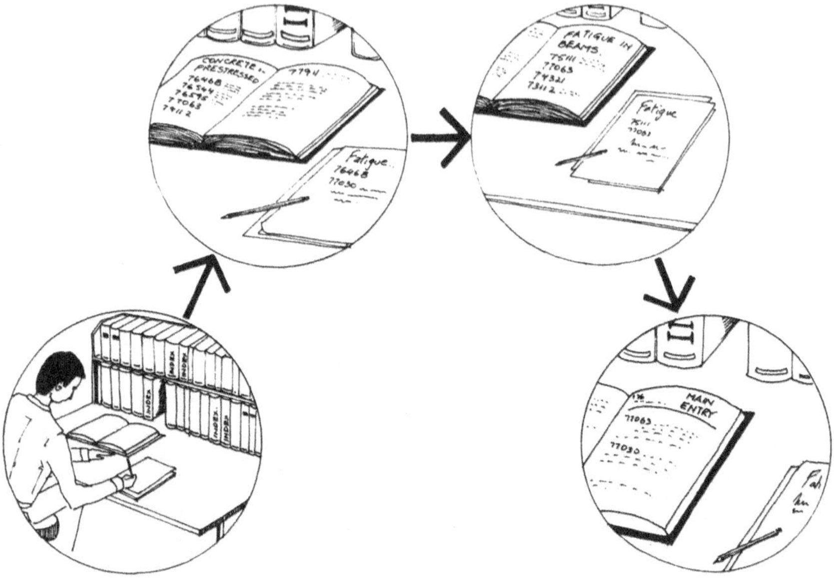

Figure 1-5. Steps in the use of a coordinate index.

In addition to the two types of printed indexes illustrated in Figures 1-4 and 1-5, coordinate indexes appear in at least two other physical forms. Peek-a-boo systems utilize gridded cards with document numbers represented by punched holes. Coordination of terms is effected by overlaying cards on a brightly colored board or light table and relevant items are then identified by the spots of color or light appearing where holes in the cards align. The fourth type of coordinate index is the permuted term display, found in works such as *Science Citation Index* or *Social Sciences Citation Index,* both published by the Institute for Scientific Information. Permuted indexes display for the reader related word pairs. The example in Figure 1-6 shows a listing of title words appearing together with the word "lifelong." Thus an educator interested in the concept of lifelong learning might want to turn to the sixth, tenth, and eighteenth items in the list which mention "curriculum," "education," or "learning" in conjunction with the term "lifelong."

HEALTHIER - - FLEMENBA A
INDIVIDUAL - RAMSHAW JE
INDUSTRIES - MOLTENI C+
JUVENILE - - ◆WEINER AJ+
LARGE - - - - MOLTENI C+
MEMBERS - - MCEVOY L
MISSOURI - - - "
PATHWAY - - - FLEMENBA A
PATTERNS - - MCEVOY L
PREFERENCES THOMPSON KS
PREVENTING - TIMBERLA EM
PROBABILITY - COHEN LE
PSYCHIATRI - FLEMENBA A
PSYCHOPATH - GIOVACCH PL
REACTIVITY - - LOVALLO WR
REDUCTION - - GYNTELBE F
RESIDENT - - - LOVALLO WR
RESPONSE - - RAMSHAW JE
RLDS - - - - - MCEVOY L
SINGLE - - - - REISTER BW
SOCIOCULTU - GIOVACCH PL
STUDY - - - - MOLTENI C+
- - - - REISTER BW
SURGERY - - - RAMSHAW JE
TIME - - - - - ARNDT J
UNDERGRADU POPE HG
UNIVERSITY - THOMPSON KS
USE - - - - - ARNDT J
VALUES - THOMPSON KS
VICTIMIZAT - COHEN LE
VIOLENT - - - WEINER AJ+
WHITE-COLL - MOLTENI C+
WORKERS - - - "+

LIFE-STYLES
ADULT - - - ◆STEWART AJ
ALTERNATIVE ◆NADELSON C
APPRAISAL - ◆HURLBURT G
AUSTRALIAN ◆BAGGS SA
CANADIAN - - HURLBURT G
CATECHOLAM ◆REYNOLDS V
CHILDREN - - - NADELSON C
DEPRESSION - STEWART AJ
EXCRETION - - REYNOLDS V
EXPERIENCES ◆GAGNON JH+
FACILITATI - ◆LLOYD GA+
- ◆ROSEN H+
GAY - - - - - - GAGNON JH+
GHETTO - - - ◆GILKES CT+
GUIDE - - - - - LLOYD GA+
- - - - - - ROSEN H+
HEALTH - - - ◆BERLINGU G
HIGH-SCHOOL - HURLBURT G
ILLNESS - - - STEWART AJ
LEISURE - - ◆GLYPTIS SA
LESBIANS - - - GAGNON JH+
LIFE - - - - - - STEWART AJ
MALE-POPUL - REYNOLDS V
MEN - - - - - GAGNON JH+
MENTAL-HEA NADELSON C
NEW - - - - - BAGGS SA
- - - - ◆KITAGAWA EM
OTMOOR - - - - REYNOLDS V
OXFORDSHIRE "
PLANNING - ◆SACHS I
POSITIVE - - - LLOYD GA+
- - - ROSEN H+

LIFELINE
BLOCK - - - ◆NEUFELD JL
CONSUMPTION "
DEVICE - - - ◆BURGESS G
ELECTRICITY - "
- NEUFELD JL
INCOME - - - - BURGESS G
INFLATION - ◆MOSER ST
INVERTED - - - NEUFELD JL
MICRO-EFFI - "
RATES - - - - BURGESS G
- - - - NEUFELD JL
TRANSFER - - BURGESS G

LIFELONG
ADAPTATION ◆BECKER G
AMERICA - - ◆DELDIN B+
CHAUTAUQUA ◆STUBBLEF HW
COMMUNITY ◆KIDD JR+
CREATIVITI - ◆FORQUIN JC+
CURRICULUM ◆MILLIKAN RH+
DEAF - - - - - BECKER G
DELPHI - - - ◆HARRIS MH+
DIALECTIC - ◆ADAMS V
EDUCATION - - FOPQUIN JC+
- ◆HIEMSTRA R+
- ◆KIDD JR@+
◆LENGRAND P+
◆LUCKHAM B+
- - MILLIKAN RH+
- ◆PARSONS PM+
FIGHT - - - - ◆BISINSKI JT
FUTURE - - - - KIDD JR+
GELPI - - - - - "+
HANDBOOK - - PARSONS PM+
IDEA - - - - - STUBBLEF HW
INTEGRATION - MILLIKAN RH+
INTERDEPEN - FORQUIN JC+
LEARNING - ◆CREAGER JG@
- ◆CROPLEY AJ
- - DELDIN B+
- - HARRIS MH+
- - KIDD JR+
- - LUCKHAM B+
- ◆PITTMAN V+
- - STUBBLEF HW
LOVE-HATE - - ADAMS V
MOVEMENT - - STUBBLEF HW
PEOPLE - - - - BECKER G
POLAND - - - - BISINSKI JT
PUBLIC-LIB - - HARRIS MH+
PURSUIT - - - CREAGER JG@
RECURRENT - - LUCKHAM B+
STUDY - - - - HARRIS MH+
SYSTEM - - - - HIEMSTRA R+
VIEW - - - - - KIDD JR+

LIFES
HALF - - - - ◆SOLER MA+
LESSONS - - ◆FULLER P

LIFESAVING
AUTONOMY - ◆MILLER BL
REFUSAL - - - "
TREATMENT - "

Figure 1-6. Permuted title word index from Social Sciences Citation Index (Philadelphia: Institute for Scientific Information), 1981.

Computer Retrieval Systems

Although coordinate indexes in printed form can be extremely helpful in library research, they quickly lose their usefulness when the number of items to be indexed exceeds a few hundred or when the number of terms to be coordinated becomes large. When these limits are reached, the physical task of comparing large lists of document tags or manipulating a dozen or more search terms simultaneously is one that only the hardiest of readers is prepared to undertake. Computers, on the other hand, are ideally suited for performing these tasks. It is precisely this set of operations that form the basis of online *retrieval* systems in operation today. In a matter of seconds the computer transcribes hundreds of document tags into the active workspace of a user and, when instructed, can quickly compare any set of tags with any number of other sets of tags to identify references meeting the reader's needs.

Thus with a computer-based retrieval system it becomes easy for a library researcher to search indexes using a logical profile of a dozen or more words and phrases that are to be grouped together in several ways. The product resulting from such a search would very likely provide not only the relevant citations that the researcher could have found with a manual search, but also a number of references that are on target but may have been missed. For example, the desired terms may have appeared in papers slanted in a different direction so that the reference would have been indexed under a heading the reader may not have thought to consult. The power of the computer to search large volumes of literature rapidly and thoroughly also makes the task of reviewing literature easy enough that reseachers may choose to query indexes and abstracts they would not normally attempt with manual search techniques. The result is that when used judiciously, the computer as a library research aid has the power to improve the quality of literature reviews both by providing more thorough searches through a single index and by encouraging similar searches through additional indexes.

Constraints on Computer Systems

The improvements in library research made possible by computer systems are not without their concomitant costs. The limitations and drawbacks to computer literature searching fall into the categories of coverage, economics, and structure. The first two categories are fairly straightforward problems. Since the technology for building computerized bibliographic files did not develop until the late sixties, most of the machine-readable indexing and abstracting files go back only to the point that their producers adopted computer technology in their editorial operations. Users of such a system simply have to decide whether a computer search of the literature for the time period for which the file is available will fulfill their needs. In some instances the computer search of current literature may need to be supplemented with a manual review of older work. On the other hand, if the topic of interest is quite new, a search covering only the most recent eight to ten years may be fully adequate.

Insofar as costs are concerned, a researcher's economic situation—either organizational or personal—may bear on his decision to use a computer search service. The pricing of computer literature searches today is typically based on interaction time, the amount of time one's terminal is physically in connection with the search service computer. If it takes fifteen minutes for a terminal operator to key in a search strategy and manipulate the results so that optimal results are achieved, then a bill for a quarter of an hour's use of the computer resource will be generated. Hourly rates vary widely, from around $22 per hour for off-peak time use of a file such as the National Library of Medicine's MEDLINE database to $100 per hour or more for a legal research file such as WESTLAW. Particularly where hourly connect charges are high, the user may choose to order delayed printouts of the results of the search in order to reduce the overall cost of the search. When such an option is exercised, there is usually an additional charge per citation or per page printed out. In institutions where information services are paid for as a part of research overhead, the actual cost of a computer literature search may not enter into a researcher's decision-making process. Where all or part of such a service is charged back to the user—either as a direct personal charge or a charge to the research budget—cost decisions may weigh heavily in the choice of method of conducting library research.

Although time coverage and cost of service bear significantly on one's decision whether to use a computer search service, they are factors that can be considered quite separately from the content and structure of the computer database itself. Either the time span covered and the potential cost justify conducting a search or they don't. When one considers the structural limitations of computer search systems, however, the problem becomes much more complex. There are the obvious and ever-present limitations arising from the way a machine can combine terms or the way a particular service has chosen to create its machine-readable file. There are also a multitude of terminological and syntactic problems arising from the way individuals communicate both as professionals in a technical field and simply as human beings. Developing strategies to overcome the limitations posed by the elements in this third category presents the greatest challenge in producing a successful product from a computer search. Indeed, the development of such strategies will be a significant theme throughout the discipline-specific chapters that follow.

2
The Researcher–Search Analyst Partnership

Before turning to databases and research strategies for specific fields of research, we may find it helpful to review how computer search services have come to be administered in most organizations. In particular we need to consider the working relationships that appear to have evolved between researchers and the information specialists who have become the usual intermediaries for computer searching of literature.

In the early days of computer literature-retrieval systems there was a good deal of talk about "end-user" operation of terminals. System designers felt that engineers, scientists, and others who sought information in bibliographic sources—that is, the ultimate users of search results—would be the people who constructed search strategies and operated the computer terminals. This scenario has simply not been played out in many organizations as of the early 1980s.

There are a number of reasons why end users have not become actively involved in computer literature searching to any great extent. From the researcher's perspective the inhibiting factors fall into three main categories: system complexity, database complexity, and search costs. The searching protocols, the instructions required for computer communications, have changed frequently over the past decade. The sheer growth in numbers and the structural complexity of many of the databases requires a great deal of effort by the user of the system in order to get the best results from a search in the most efficient manner. The charging system used by most online computer services, where the cost of service is directly related to the length of time that the user is physically in connection with the computer, puts the infrequent user at a disadvantage in that his searches may very well cost a great deal more than they might simply because he is slower in using the system. Few scientists are eager to spend their research money at $60 to $100 per hour to operate a system that they use only infrequently, especially if an expert in system use, willing to act as an intermediary, can provide the service at a lower total cost.

The pattern that has evolved in most organizations is for staff members in the library or information center to act as the interface between computer search services and researchers. In the last decade a new job title has emerged as a result of this intermediary role; a "search analyst" is an information specialist or librarian with training in the construction and execution of strategies to retrieve information via computer. These specialists have accepted this job as a logical extension of their traditional role as providers of information from printed resources. Because of their general familiarity with the content and structure of reference tools and their generally more expert knowledge of system protocols gained through frequent use, search analysts at the present time can usually provide more thorough and cost-effective searches than end users can provide for themselves through direct searching of files online.

Because most searches today are conducted by intermediaries, a special partnership has developed between the requesters and the providers of computer literature searches. Each plays a vital role in the success of the search. The requester provides the substance of the inquiry—the question, the limitations, knowledge about the field to be searched, and terminology current in that field. The search analyst, usually trained in library or information science, brings to the process a knowledge about the content and structure of information retrieval tools, familiarity with indexing vocabularies, and skill in constructing and executing search strategies online.

In highly specialized research institutions, search analysts may have extensive subject background in the areas to be searched as well. In such an organization the end user may need only state the need for a literature review and the search analyst can complete the task without further assistance from the requester.

TOPIC: Creativity in Minority Children.

Concept 1	Concept 2	Concept 3	Concept 4
Creativ(e,ity)	Minor(ity,ities)	Child(ren)	YR=1980
Art(istic)	Black(s)	Boy(s)	YR=1981
Music(al)	Hispan(o,ic,ics)	Girl(s)	YR=1982
Divergent	Mexican American		
Thinking	Mexican Americans		
Divergent	Asian American		
Thought	Asian Americans		
	Native American		
	Native Americans		
	American Indian		
	American Indians		

LOGIC: (Narrow) Concept 1 AND Concept 2 AND Concept 3 AND Concept 4
(Broad) Concept 1 AND Concept 2 AND Concept 4

Figure 2-1. Strategy for search on creativity.

More typically, however, the search analyst will not be a specialist in all areas for which computer searches are needed, and so will need to rely on the requester for assistance in selection of terms to go into the strategy or search profile. The researcher will therefore need to be present during the online session in order to get feedback during the course of the interaction with the computer. Ideally the relationship between the search analyst and the end user of information is a synergistic one, resulting in the best retrieval possible. The searcher-requester interaction typically has three distinct phases. During the inquiry phase the requester states the topic of interest and the search analyst may explain a bit about the principles, capabilities, and limitations of the literature search system or systems available to them. During this phase the analyst will help the requester select the databases most appropriate for the topic. Once the topic to be searched has been explained and the files to be searched are selected, the profiling phase begins. As explained in Chapter 1, coordinate indexing systems are based on the co-occurrence of strings of characters within specific parts or fields of a bibliographic citation. The profile is a written outline of character strings—words, phrases, special codes, etc.—grouped in such a way as to identify relevant references. Figure 2-1 shows a profile that might be used to query a psychological database for recent information on creativity in minority children. It shows that each major element implicit in the topic (concepts 1, 2, and 3) could be represented in a citation that would be interesting to the requester by any of several synonymous terms, either single words or multi-word phrases. The search elements can be words that might show up in titles or summaries as in the first three concepts, or they can be other relevant restricters such as the publication dates listed in concept 4. Terms within each concept listing are considered to be equally acceptable alternatives, that is, if any one of them appears in the citation, the requirements of that concept will be satisfied. The profile indicates that two combinations of the concept groupings are contemplated. First, all four groups would be intersected with the goal of finding references to the topic as originally stated. A second combination of the concepts for creativity, minorities, and date are also suggested as a check to see what has been written on minority creativity without specific mention of children. Contingency planning such as that suggested by the alternative combination of concepts is a common practice in profile construction since the computer can "see" only specific character strings. Because of this limitation, a search strategy defined very narrowly (i.e., *all* concepts in the original request must be met) may miss some potentially useful references. Less restrictive combinations can frequently produce valuable information, particularly where the volume of literature to be retrieved is not large to begin with.

Once the profile is completed, the search analyst then logs onto the computer system and enters the strategy. After the desired combinations of search elements are made, the analyst usually will have a sample of the results typed out in order to check the quality of the answer set, that is, the group of references identified by the computer as containing the search terms in the combinations specified. If the sample appears sufficiently relevant to the question, a printout of the complete list of references can be requested. However, this straightforward sequence of typing terms, checking results, and requesting printouts does not always suffice. The search analyst often must make further modifications to search results during this third phase of the process. Given the proclivities of language to take unexpected turns that can confuse communication in a computerized environment, a sampling of search results may reveal that a large number of irrelevant references have been retrieved through the appearance of a word or phrase used in an unexpected way. For example, a search for information on the economics of the boating industry may have requested to see references with, among others, the terms "economy" and "boat" in them. While these words are clear and precise in the context of the question being asked, it is altogether possible for the computer to retrieve a number of articles from a general business database that contain the terms used metaphorically, such as the title, "The Elephant in the Boat: The United States and the World Economy."

Even without semantic problems of this sort, numerous problems of a similar nature are discovered only when a sample of references is taken during the search session. It is at this point that the requester can be of invaluable assistance. While some problems of semantics and metaphorical usage such as the "economic boat" may have to be accepted, other terminological problems can be effectively dealt with by a person thoroughly familiar with the problem to which the information will be applied. Perhaps a high percentage of the items originally retrieved discuss applications in an area off-target for the problem being studied. The requester may be able to provide additional terminology that will enable the search analyst to refine the answer set so that relevance is increased. In other instances, where relevance is not a problem but the volume of information is too great, the requester can easily provide the criteria necessary for producing a more manageable result—perhaps by providing an arbitrary number of references or by establishing priorities as to which aspects of the topic should be emphasized.

As computer retrieval systems become more "user-friendly," the pattern of searches being conducted primarily by trained intermediaries will almost certainly shift to one in which increasing numbers of scientists and scholars will conduct their own online literature reviews. But even as those systems evolve, the assistance available from information specialists can be valuable to the researcher—whether they act as the intermediary actually retrieving information online or as a counselor in database selection and profile construction.

The remaining chapters in this book are designed to assist the end users of information in two ways. If they are using a mediated service, that is, one in which the search is profiled and conducted by a search analyst, it will help them to understand more fully the databases available in their field of research and to be alert to the kinds of information the search analyst may need to know in order to retrieve the best possible results. For the end users who plan to profile and conduct their own searches, it will serve as an expanded guide to file selection and database features that they must master in order to retrieve the most relevant information from the resources available to them.

3
Agricultural and Life Sciences

Characteristics and Terminology

Literature resources for the study of agricultural and life sciences are among the richest and most diverse of any field. They encompass all major types of publications from patents and technical reports to monographic treatises and journal articles. The subject matter of interest to life scientists is equally diverse, covering topics ranging from improved electrophoretic techniques to population studies of waterfowl, from the taxonomy of Lepidoptera species to the epidemiology of Legionnaire's Disease.

In this field, specialties and subspecialties abound to such an extent that any attempts at disciplinary classification inevitably fail. For purposes of discussion here the fields usually subsumed by the following academic departments will be included: Animal Science, Plant Science, Entomology, Biology, Biochemistry, Biophysics, Human and Veterinary Medicine, Forest Science, Food Science, Soil Science, and Agronomy. Bibliographic tools for control of the literature in these fields abound at several levels of specificity. Large, general purpose abstracting and indexing services such as *Biological Abstracts* and *Science Citation Index* cover the major publications of the life sciences very broadly, while other services such as *Herbage Abstracts, Microbiology Abstracts,* and *Reviews of Applied Entomology* cover in more detail the publications of specific subdisciplines.

With a few notable exceptions, most of the major indexes and abstracting services can be searched via computer for references published during the past several years. Given the history of computer search systems, the time span covered by individual online versions of these bibliographic services will vary, but the typical system will cover the literature of the past five to ten years, with a few services extending coverage back as far as the mid-1960s. Time coverage will frequently be a factor in a scientist's decision whether or not to undertake a computer search. If the topic under investigation is one in which a substantial volume of the relevant literature has been written in the last decade, then a computer search can be an effective aid to the library research. New research areas such as genetic engineering and space medicine will be particularly well served by computer-searchable systems. Other fields—many of the plant and animal science specialties, for example—in which the research output has been relatively steady over a long period of time will also be well served by computer searching. In this latter case the researcher may choose to search current literature online, realizing that although the results will not be a complete search of the published record, good citations retrieved by the search will likely have bibliographic references to key papers published in the past. In this manner a thorough search of the most recent ten years of literature may yield results that, in effect, give coverage of fifteen to twenty years of significant research.

In other instances, however, computer searching may not prove to be of so much value. Taxonomic work, for example, requires investigations going well beyond the decade or so that computers can search, and frequently valuable taxonomic information is to be found in brief notes or professional communications that usually provide no further bibliographic leads. In fields where the research effort has not been continuous, the discontinuity may also pose problems for computer searching. This is particularly true in instances where substantial work was conducted, say, thirty years ago and then for some reason discontinued. The researcher who now wants to resume such a line of investigation will certainly want to review the early literature, but a computer search will very likely provide little help unless others who have also renewed their interest in the field have perhaps published recent reviews of the literature. Illustrative of this category is much of the work on alternate energy resources, on some of the crops suitable for marginal lands, and on insect pests or diseases that tend to pose major problems in rather long cyclic patterns.

As the disciplines subsumed under the heading of agricultural and life sciences exhibit wide diversity so do their information resources. At one extreme are tools such as the National Library of Medicine's *Index Medicus* (online called MEDLINE) and Chemical Abstracts Service's *Chemical Abstracts* (CA SEARCH online) in which indexing is controlled through extensive vocabulary tools and thesauri. Because of the extra effort that these organizations have expended on file creation and vocabulary control, searchers using these resources can achieve highly precise results, but they must in turn be willing to expend extra effort to master the tools available for constructing effective profiles and to understand the rather complex structure of some of the bibliographic records. At the other extreme one finds resources such as the National Agricultural Library's AGRICOLA database and the Institute for Scientific Information's *Science Citation Index* (SCISEARCH) in which heavy reliance is placed on the titles of references to provide access terminology. Such databases have the advantage of quickness in preparation of citations in that references are not delayed for elaborate indexing and abstracting, but searchers must be aware in choosing to search such files that consistency in access terminology is no longer available to the degree that it is in a more heavily indexed resource. They must, therefore, compensate by adding to their information profile alternative terms that might appear in the titles of relevant references. For example, in the MEDLINE system the term "cattle" will be applied to all items in that database dealing with those animals, but in the SCISEARCH database users will have to include all possible names for cattle—cow, cows, calf, calves, steers, etc.

Terminological pitfalls abound in many of the databases, particularly those covering several disciplines. For example, the computer database of the Commonwealth Agricultural Bureaux (CAB) consists of the machine-readable equivalents of nearly three dozen different indexing and abstracting publications, ranging in content from plant breeding to veterinary medicine. Thus, researchers needing information on digestion in cattle may find articles in their search output on anaerobic digestion of waste products in cattle feedlots. Usually the context created by other terms in the search strategy helps to eliminate the vast majority of irrelevancies or "false hits," but it is virtually impossible to imagine all possible uses to which some of the more common words will be put. Narrowly defined fields with a highly specific vocabulary usually are less prone to this type of terminological problem than are applied fields in which concepts are often borrowed from many disciplines. Even the disciplines with relatively "pure" terminology, however, can present monumental problems for online searching, particularly when there is more than one standard method for describing, classifying, or naming substances and/or phenomena. Consider, for example, the various ways that a relatively simple compound such as isopropyl alcohol might be known in the literature of organic chemistry:

Isopropyl Alcohol
- 2-propanol
- Isopropanol
- Secondary propyl alcohol
- Dimethyl carbinol
- Petrohol

Many of the database producers and the online search systems themselves now provide powerful searching features that can help overcome a number of the problems. In some instances additional intellectual effort is expended in creating record elements that will make easier the task of searching troublesome topics, and in other cases additional online programs and search aids can sort quickly through masses of data. The user must, however, bear in mind that these search features have usually evolved over the recent life of the databases and may not be available throughout the entire database. This problem is heightened by the fact that most online versions of databases are built incrementally from periodically issued update tapes. As policies and procedures change, the records on the tape change as well, so that an effective search must take into account these changes over time.

An excellent example of this latter sort of problem is exhibited by the AGRICOLA database of the National Agricultural Library. Over the course of AGRICOLA's life as a machine-readable file beginning in 1970, there have been numerous policy changes within the National Agricultural Library itself, and into the file have been incorporated computerized records from other organizations that have had their own policies in formatting bibliographic records. As a result searchers of that database not only must know the terminology of the field in which they are conducting the literature review but also need to be aware of the history of the database itself. There are, for example, no fewer than six different major subject category schemes that have governed the indexing of substantial numbers of bibliographic citations in the database. Users who are not aware of this fact may inadvertently use one of the codes, retrieve good results, and think that they have found all the relevant papers in the database on the topic, when in fact they have missed dozens of relevant citations that were coded using one of the other five schemes.

The idiosyncrasies of databases will prove irksome to some, dismaying to others. Not all the potential problems can be foreseen by even the most adept search analyst, but time spent in perusing database documentation and in gaining familiarity with the tools and techniques outlined in the next section should make the task of profile construction a good deal easier.

Profiling Assistance

1 Substances

Chemical substances, particularly those in living systems, pose a number of problems for researchers trying to conduct computer literature reviews. The amount of assistance available for profile construction varies widely among databases. The features described below are indicative of the resources that may be tapped in profiling. Certainly not all features will be available in every database.

CAS Registry Numbers. In 1965 the Chemical Abstracts Service of the American Chemical Society began to catalog and assign unique registry numbers to the substances described or reported in the literature it indexed. Over the intervening eighteen years this registry has grown to include more than 5,000,000 substances. Although a great deal of time continues to be spent devising standard systems of nomenclature, a great deal of variation continues to exist in the proper names applied to substances. The registry number provides the searcher many advantages, but most notable are its uniqueness and its brevity. A new registry number is assigned to each new compound reported in chemical literature without respect to any classification scheme. The numbers are not, therefore, subject to changing trends in chemical nomenclature. Numbers are changed from time to time, but these changes are a result of new knowledge about the nature of the compound and not merely of shifts in naming conventions. The uniqueness of the numbers increases the probability that searchers will be able to find all papers on a given compound without worrying that they have missed references to one of its many synonyms or have failed to match character-for-character the exact name of the compound as it appears in the database they are searching.

The brevity of registry numbers (usually no more than nine or ten characters, including hyphens) compared to their spelled out equivalents aids both index producer and database searcher. Because they are short, registry numbers allow shorter physical bibliographic records; so more information can be stored in less space. Some searchers may argue that typing numbers is more exacting work than typing words, but it is generally true that a registry number can be entered online more quickly than the equivalent substance name. Most certainly it represents far less effort to type than does the entry of all variations that the name of a substance may have. To illustrate, the entry below shows the name variations associated with the compound chloroprene:

Chloroprene
  2-chloror-1,3,butadiene
  Chlorobutadiene
  CBD
  2-chloro-1,3,butadiene

Beta chloroprene
2-chlorobuta-1,3 diene
Registry Number: 126-99-8

For those who must find registry numbers for substances, there are many sources. Among the most valuable printed sources for this purpose are the following:

- *Merck Index,* 9th ed. (Rahway, N.J.: Merck & Co., 1976). Though by no means complete, the *Merck Index* does provide a useful list of the most common compounds. Entries include molecular formula, *Chemical Abstracts* name, synonyms, and structural diagrams. In a separate appendix *Merck* also lists CAS registry numbers for several thousand compounds, which makes this a convenient single-volume tool to have close to the computer terminal for profiling help.
- *Chemical Abstracts Index Guide* (Columbus, Ohio: Chemical Abstracts Service). This guide to the terminology used in *Chemical Abstracts* alerts the user to the proper form of chemical names and provides registry numbers for the substances indexed.
- *Toxic Substances Control Act Chemical Substance Inventory* (Washington, D.C.: U. S. Environmental Protection Agency, 1979). This multi-volume inventory provides name, formula, and CAS registry number indexes to 44,000 chemical substances known to be in U. S. commerce (production, imports, exports, etc.). Toxicity is *not* a criterion for listing in the inventory. Excluded from the inventory are pesticides, food products, tobacco products, food additives, drugs, and cosmetics. It does include "naturally occurring" chemical substances, those substances in nature that exist in unprocessed form or are produced by purely manual, mechanical, or gravitational means, through dissolution in water, or through the application only of heat to remove water.

Online sources are also readily available. In most cases the online nomenclature files are the equivalents of printed tools, but they provide searching capabilities far beyond printed resources. Frequently, a scientist needs to find literature on entire classes of compounds—all substances with one selenium atom plus an alkane group, for example. The amount of effort that would be required to find all such compounds would be monumental, but online chemical dictionaries such as CHEMLINE, CHEMDEX, and CHEMSIS make the task an easy one. Some systems even provide the automatic transcription of relevant registry numbers into a search strategy, thereby avoiding for the terminal operator the burden of typing in those numbers.

Enzyme Commission Numbers. Like registry numbers, the numbers created by the Enzyme Commission of the International Union of Pure and Applied Chemistry and the International Union of Biochemistry provide a unique method of identifying specific enzymes without having to type in full names and synonyms for these compounds. The printed tools most helpful in locating Enzyme Commission numbers are the following:

- *Enzyme Nomenclature, 1978,* by The Nomenclature Committee of the International Union of Biochemistry. (New York: Academic Press, 1979). This volume lists Enzyme Commission numbers, recommended names, and synonyms for over 2,100 enzymes.
- *Medical Subject Headings—Supplementary Chemical Records, 1983.* (Bethesda, MD: National Library of Medicine, 1983). A guide to official names, synonyms, and the medical subject headings employed by indexers for *Index Medicus,* this volume also provides CAS registry numbers and Enzyme Commission numbers for approximately 25,000 compounds.

Established Names. Not every database, of course, has included unique substance numbers for the compounds it indexes, so those who write profiles to search these files must include the names. Nomenclature can vary widely; some compounds will have but a single name recognized by everyone in the field, while others present a bewildering array of names. In the latter case, there may be several formalized names created according to varying naming conventions. In addition there may also be numerous common names (e.g., aspirin, vinegar, alum) and/or trade names (particularly among biologics and other commercially important compounds).

When faced with the task of profiling a search that must include the actual names of compounds, as in, for example, a search of the National Agricultural Library's AGRICOLA database, a researcher needs to spend some time with tools such as the *Merck Index* and the *Chemical Abstracts Index Guide.* For pharmaceutical compounds and biomedically important substances the National Library of Medicine's *Medical Subject Headings* (*MeSH*) is also a valuable reference. The alphabetical portion of this standard indexing tool for medical literature provides numerous established names and cross references, while the hierarchical section (tree structures) provides a convenient classified arrangement of terms grouped conceptually. A researcher interested in catecholamines could, with *MeSH,* look up that group of substances and quickly find a list of specific substances belonging to that class to add to a word strategy.

Specialized catalogs and chemical dictionaries in both printed and computerized forms can also be helpful in identifying synonyms and variant names for compounds. The catalogs of major chemical firms as well as the numerous lists of compounds for specialized groups of chemicals such as agricultural chemicals or pesticides will provide assistance not only in determining variant "official" names but also in locating commonly used trade names. The online chemical dictionary files, already discussed in relation to registry numbers, also contain information about variant names and synonyms that have been identified by chemical indexers.

The researchers' own experience and the nature of the field of inquiry in which they work are also significant factors in selecting search profile terms. When several names for the same compound are encountered, researchers may recognize some of them as being in more common usage in their discipline. For example, papers dealing with application and performance testing of a herbicide such as "Roundup" may very well use just that trade name, while research dealing with laboratory investigations on its residual effects and toxicity might be likely to report results by citing a name such as "glyphosate" or "n-(phosphomethyl) glycine, isopropylamine salt." As this example illustrates, although some searches will require the entry of all possible synonyms for substances, the context or the slant of the question being asked may allow a more selective choice for search terms.

2 Organisms

Conventions for the formal naming of living things have been long established. When used with care, these names can identify organisms with great precision. Research reports, however, frequently fail to reflect as careful a use of biosystematic names as one would like, and this shortcoming creates problems for those searching the literature. Perhaps the greatest problem faced in profiling searches for particular organisms is that of common names versus genus-species names. It is a two-edged sword: A single common name may be applied widely to several species in the same genus—or even to very different organisms—or, conversely, several common names may have currency for a single species. When the literature fails to identify the organisms studied, the percentage of relevant references retrieved by the online search will inevitably decline.

Practices in naming of organisms in plant research reports vary by research specialty. Agronomists working with common economic crops will very likely use common names such as corn or wheat in preference to the scientific names *Zea mays* or *Triticum aestivum.* Geneticists, botanists, taxonomic specialists, and others working in areas where species or varietal differences are of major significance will be more likely to include the scientific names in what they write.

Similar problems exist for animal researchers. Those dealing with highly speciated groups will generally report scientific names; those working with more common organisms—particularly if they are economically important (cattle, sheep, etc.)—will use common names. In animal science research, however, even common names pose the additional problem of what can be called "implicit class names," that is, multiple names for the same creature denoting its sex and/or stage of development. For example, articles on cattle might very well contain any of the following terms: "cow," "bull," "calf," "heifer," "steer," "bovine," or "cattle," plus the plurals of many of these terms. Genetics and animal breeding papers occasionally further complicate matters by simply referring to specific breeds, as in the title "Performance of Grass-fed Jersey × Simmental Crosses," taking for granted that readers would know immediately that the subject was cattle, as indeed they would. The computer, on the other hand, holds none of the store of knowledge that the human reader does, so profiles need to be structured to compensate for this failing of the machine. Some abstracting and indexing systems do compensate for the variability that can occur in the literature by assigning standardized keywords to citations, but many others do not, leaving to the scholar the task of searching as many of the possible word variations as might be considered relevant.

Printed tools such as the biosystematic code section in the *BIOSIS Search Guide* can be helpful when search requirements are broad enough to include entire orders of organisms (e.g., all Lepidoptera). Standard classification guides will be necessary when a finer delineation of genera and species is required. Among the wealth of tools that exist in this area, the following is particularly helpful:

- *Synopsis and Classification of Living Organisms* (New York: McGraw-Hill, 1982). 2 volumes. The bulk of this work contains descriptions of major taxonomic groups of plants and animals, each with bibliographic references to sources of more detailed classification. The most useful features of the work for search strategy construction are the forty-six page classification and the index to the set, both in volume two. The classification provides a hierarchical taxonomic display through the family level, and the index provides access to scientific and common names of thousands of organisms.

3 Anatomy and Structure

As biological research focuses on ever more specialized areas, new terminology develops that the library researcher must master. The researcher working within a specialty and seeking only papers in that narrow area may have little difficulty in specifying just the right terms. A colleague who is looking for literature from several specialized areas of research in order to solve an interdisciplinary problem may experience, however,

CELLS	A11
ANTIBODY PRODUCING CELLS	A11.63
B LYMPHOCYTES	A11.63.438
PLASMA CELLS	A11.63.693
APUD CELLS	A11.70
BLASTOMERES	A11.104
BLOOD CELLS	A11.118
BLOOD PLATELETS	A11.118.188
ERYTHROCYTES	A11.118.413
ERYTHROBLASTS •	A11.118.413.200
ERYTHROCYTE MEMBRANE •	A11.118.413.270
ERYTHROCYTES, ABNORMAL	A11.118.413.330
ACANTHOCYTES •	A11.118.413.330.100
ERYTHROCYTE INCLUSIONS •	A11.118.413.330.340
HEINZ BODIES	A11.118.413.330.340.335
MEGALOBLASTS •	A11.118.413.330.531
SPHEROCYTES •	A11.118.413.330.802
RETICULOCYTES	A11.118.413.730
HEMOCYTES •	A11.118.480
LEUKOCYTES	A11.118.637
GRANULOCYTES	A11.118.637.415
BASOPHILS	A11.118.637.415.120
EOSINOPHILS	A11.118.637.415.345
NEUTROPHILS	A11.118.637.415.583
LYMPHOCYTES	A11.118.637.555
KILLER CELLS	A11.118.637.555.420
KILLER CELLS, NATURAL	A11.118.637.555.425
B LYMPHOCYTES	A11.118.637.555.438

Figure 3-1. *MeSH* Tree Structure.

tremendous frustration in finding appropriate terminology for a search of the literature.

Here a good up-to-date advanced textbook may be invaluable as is a work such as *Medical Subject Headings* (*MeSH*). The textbook will be useful both in providing appropriate terminology and in identifying seminal articles in the specialty. Those articles could be retrieved online via a title-word search in order to see what terms were used to index them. By using those terms, other relevant citations might also be retrieved. *MeSH* is especially useful for investigations dealing with animal studies, particularly higher animals. The alphabetic section lists thousands of medical and biomedical terms and points the user to one or more hierarchies where displays of many narrower or broader terms can be found that may be of use to the search strategy. Figure 3-1 illustrates part of a typical *MeSH* hierarchy or tree structure.

When faced with a list of potentially relevant terms for constructing a search strategy, one must keep in mind that specificity is a characteristic sought by authors and indexers alike. If an author has conducted research on neoplasms of the duodenum, it will be that structure that is mentioned in the article title. Likewise, an indexer entering that citation into a database will assign as specific a set of descriptors to that reference as the indexing system will allow. A researcher looking for literature on neoplasms of the upper gastrointestinal tract, therefore, will be well advised to include both the phrase denoting the generalized anatomical area and the names of more specific structures within that region.

4 Approach or Focus

One of the most troublesome aspects of searching secondary tools for research literature is that of trying to identify papers using a particular approach to the problem. The methodology employed or the theoretical underpinnings of a piece of research are more often than not elements that are not discernible in index citations. Authors and indexers alike tend to focus on research results when characterizing a piece of writing, either through its title or a list of keywords. In instances where the methodology or the theoretical framework is the focus of the paper, one can expect to find terminology alluding to that fact; where the focus is elsewhere the likelihood of finding appropriate word clues is much less certain. This situation means for the library researcher that the search request may need to be re-evaluated so that additional papers on the general topic can be retrieved in the event that a narrower search profile limited to the desired techniques retrieves too few papers. For example, a search for references on brucellosis in which the rose bengal test was employed may need to be broadened to include other brucellosis studies where that test is not specified.

Aside from purely methodological studies, online searchers may need to establish a context for the search terms in the profile. For example, a plant scientist may want to review the literature on phosphate absorption among higher plants, avoiding papers dealing with animals and, insofar as possible, with lower plants. Here many of the online retrieval services provide precisely the right keys through the broad subject codes used initially for segmenting printed tools. One can, for example, use a single code number in a database such as BIOSIS to retrieve all papers dealing with accumulation and translocation in plants. By coupling that large group of references with an appropriate word profile for phosphates, one can effectively zero in on the relevant papers. Depending on the database, these codes will exhibit varying degrees of specificity and may, consequently, be of more or less use for a given request. Figure 3-2 illustrates a portion of the category-code listings for AGRICOLA and for BIOSIS. Users contemplating searches involving large conceptual groupings such as those outlined here may want to acquire database user guides that outline these codes in detail. Alternatively, they may want to consult the major segments of the printed equivalents to the databases, since the database codes usually correspond exactly with the major sections of the print tool.

Finally, the researcher may want to consider term weighting as a means of improving the focus of the search results. Bear in mind that this practice is not used in all databases, but where it is employed, the power to increase the relevance of computer-generated bibliographies is great. Term weighting means that some indicator (e.g., an asterisk) is attached to data elements such as code numbers or subject descriptors to indicate special emphasis. Figure 3-3 illustrates a BIOSIS citation in which special emphasis has been indicated for the concept codes for "Tissue Culture—Apparatus, Methods, and Media" (32500) and "Phytopathology—Diseases Caused by Fungi" (54502).

Typically a search is profiled so that all occurrences of the desired terms and codes are retrieved, and then if results need additional focusing an adjustment is made so that just the items with heavier emphasis on one or another aspect are retrieved. Although this technique can be very useful, it is not foolproof. Editorial policies may establish an arbitrary limit on the number of items in a single record that can receive weighting designators. By limiting the results to only weighted terms, the user may be cutting out some valuable items. Likewise, one must keep

AGRICOLA Codes

	1980-	1972-79
PLANT SCIENCE	F000	4005
Plant Production--General	F100	4050, 4055, 4060
Plant Production--Horticultural crops	F110	4055
Plant Production--Field Crops	F120	4050
Plant Production--Pastures and Range	F130	4050
Plant Production--Miscellaneous Crops	F140	4060
Plant Breeding and Genetics	F200	4025
Plant Ecology	F300	4015
Plant Structure and Cytology	F400	4020
Plant Nutrition	F500	4030, 4035, 4040, 4045
Plant Physiology and Biochemistry	F600	4030, 4035, 4040, 4045

BIOSIS Codes

PLANT PHYSIOLOGY, BIOCHEMISTRY & BIOPHYSICS	
Water Relations	CC51502
Temperature	CC51503
Nutrition	CC51504
Photosynthesis	CC51506
Respiration, Fermentation	CC51508
Growth, Differentiation	CC51510
Reproduction	CC51512
Growth Substances	CC51514
Light and Radiation Effects	CC51516
Electric, Magnetic and Gravitational Phenomena	CC51517
Enzymes	CC51518
Metabolism	CC51519
Translocation, Accumulation	CC51520
Chemical Constituents	CC51522
Bioluminescence	CC51523
Apparatus and Methods	CC51524
General and Miscellaneous	CC51526

Figure 3-2. AGRICOLA and BIOSIS code schemes.

```
75075145
  INFECTION OF TOBACCO NICOTIANA-TABACUM CALLUS BY PHYTOPHTHORA-PARASITICA-
-VAR-NICOTIANAE.
  DEZOETEN G A; GAARD G; HABERLACH G T; HELGESON J P
  DEP.  PLANT PATHOLOGY,   PLANT DISEASE RESISTANCE RESEARCH UNIT,  UNIV.
WISCONSIN, MADISON 53706.
  PHYTOPATHOLOGY  72 (7).  1982.  743-746.   Coden:  PHYTA
  Language:  ENGLISH
  Transmission and scanning electron microscopy was used to determine the
response of tobacco callus tissue to inoculation with P.  parasitica var.
nicotianae.  Callus resistant to Race 0 and susceptible to Race 1,   or
susceptible to Race 0 and Race 1, was used.  Within 3 h after inoculation,
zoospores from compatible and incompatible races had encysted and
germinated;  then  germ tubes of both races penetrated  callus cells.
Penetration often occurred in cells other than those on which the spores
germinated.  By  24  h,   when a hypersensitive reaction (HR) was clearly
evident in the incompatible combination,  almost all of the cells in the HR
area had collapsed,  whereas most cells  in infected areas on callus showing
the compatible reaction were still turgid.  After 48 h,  hyphae of the
compatible fungus had penetrated less than 50 cell layers, whereas those of
the incompatible fungus were limited to 5-8 cell layers.
  Descriptors:  ZOO SPORE GERMINATION TRANSMISSION ELECTRON MICROSCOPY
SCANNING ELECTRON MICROSCOPY CELL PENETRATION HYPER SENSITIVITY COLLAPSE
  Concept Codes:  ELECTRON MICROSCOPY(01058); CYTOLOGY/CYTOCHEM-PLANT(*02504);
TISS CULTURE-APPARAT,METHS,MEDIA(*32500);  PALYNOLOGY(50100);  PLANT MORPHOL,
EMBRYOL, ANATOMY(*51000);  PLANT PHYSIOL-GROWTH,DIFFERENTIAT(*51510);  PLANT
PHYSIOL-REPRODUCTION(51512);  AGRONOMY-TOBACCO CROPS(*52512); PHYTOPATHOL-
DIS BY FUNGI(*54502);PHYTOPATHOL-PARASITISM,RESISTNCE(*54514)
  Biosystematic Codes:  PHYCOMYCETES(15900); SOLANACEAE(26775)
```

Figure 3-3. BIOSIS citation illustrating the weighting of terms (asterisks) in in the Concept Code field.

ever in mind that decisions as to an author's emphasis are frequently a matter of editorial judgment; decisions that precisely fit the search needs of one scientist may appear arbitrary and inadequate for another.

Databases

The databases listed here are the most relevant ones for agricultural and life sciences research. Many of the files listed in other sections may also prove useful. For example, references on the teaching of life sciences subjects will be covered in the ERIC database, described in Chapter 4, and many articles on computer applications for agriculture can be found in engineering databases such as INSPEC in Chapter 5.

AGRICOLA (Beltsville, MD: U.S. Department of Agriculture, National Agricultural Library). 1,500,000 citations, 1970–

The computerized version of the USDA's *Bibliography of Agriculture* and the *Monthly Catalog of the National Agricultural Library* covers all areas of agricultural research and practice. Journals, monographs, conference proceedings, and government publications in over fifty languages are scanned for indexing. The file is particularly strong in plant sciences, animal husbandry, and agricultural economics and management. Most citations lack abstracts, and retrieval from the file relies heavily on authors' titles. Subject category codes are available for searching large subdivisions of the database. The *AGRICOLA Users Guide* will provide profiling assistance.

Alcohol Use-Abuse Database (Minneapolis, MN: University of Minnesota, Drug Information Services). 12,000 citations, 1968–1979

This file contains references to articles, reprints, papers and book chapters covering research in the causes of and treatment for chemical dependency on alcohol. Materials include both therapy for alcohol abusers and counseling for their families. Since 1980 materials on alcohol use and abuse have been entered into the DRUGINFO database.

AQUACULTURE (Rockville, MD: National Oceanic and Atmospheric Administration, Environmental Science Information Center). 5,000 citations, 1970–

All aspects of growing organisms in freshwater, brackish, and marine environments are covered, including economic and management issues. Coverage encompasses international literature in all print formats.

AQUALINE (Medmenham, Bucks, England: Water Research Centre). 26,000 citations, 1974–

International serial and monographic literature on water and aquatic environments is contained in this file, produced by the British Water Research Centre. Major areas of coverage are water treatment and quality, water resource development and management, and organisms in the aquatic environment.

Aquatic Sciences and Fisheries Abstracts (Rome: Food and Agriculture Organization of the United Nations). 85,000 citations, 1978–

Biological, physical, legal, and social aspects of oceanic and limnological environments are covered. Journals, books, conference proceedings, and technical report literature are included from a worldwide body of publications.

BIOSIS Previews (Philadelphia, PA: BioSciences Information Service). 3,500,000 citations, 1969–

The file contains all the references published since 1969 in *Biological Abstracts* and *Biological Abstracts/RRM* (formerly *Bio-Research Index*). Research journals, proceedings, and monographic works from around the world are selected for indexing. All aspects of biological and biochemical research are covered. Each citation is indexed for specific organism, larger taxonomic groups, and major systematic or research concepts. Abstracts of up to 150 words are available in most online versions of the file for records created since the mid-1970s. Numeric codes corresponding to specific taxonomic groups are available for searching. Searchers must be aware that titles are edited in order to increase retrievability of some classes of substances or organisms. Thus one will find words such as "zooplankton" or "organophosphates" edited so that they appear as "zoo plankton" and "organo phosphates." The *BIOSIS Search Guide* is necessary for good searching of this file.

CA SEARCH (Columbus, OH: Chemical Abstracts Service). 5,300,000 citations, 1967–

This massive database contains all citations and indexing in the printed volumes of *Chemical Abstracts.* All areas of chemical and biochemical research are covered, including agricultural chemicals, biochemistry, pharmacodynamics, and other areas of chemistry touching on living systems. Abstract numbers are provided, but the text of the abstracts is not included. Most online systems load CA Search records in such a way as to facilitate the searching of varying word forms. Nevertheless, the searcher must also include registry numbers and numerous abbreviations to achieve thorough retrieval from the file. The

Index Guide volumes of *Chemical Abstracts* will provide great assistance in profiling.

CAB (Slough, England: Commonwealth Agricultural Bureaux). 1,200,000 citations, 1972–

An international database, this file corresponds to the more than two dozen indexing and abstracting services of the Commonwealth Agricultural Bureaux, such as *Animal Breeding Abstracts, Weed Abstracts, Veterinary Bulletin,* and *Reviews of Applied Entomology.* Each record is indexed with terms from a controlled vocabulary and with subject codes. Most of the citations are also supplied with abstracts of up to 150 words. Searchers must bear in mind the British origin of this database and construct their profiles to accommodate both British usage and spelling conventions. Because so many different indexes have been merged in this file, the user will frequently experience a relatively high rate of "noise" in his search results. Limiting retrieval to the occurrence of terms in titles and keyword fields may be advisable as a means of reducing search results to a more manageable size. The *CAB Online Search Guide* can provide help in focusing results.

Chemical Exposure (Oak Ridge, TN: Oak Ridge National Laboratory, Chemical Effects Information Center). 4,000 records, 1974–

Providing both bibliographic references and hard data, this file enables the searcher to find quickly information on properties, variant names, known effects, and other facts related to approximately 575 chemical substances. The file is prepared by the Chemical Effects Information Center at Oak Ridge National Laboratory, and corresponds to the following publications: *Chemicals Identified in Human Biological Media* (since 1978) and *Chemicals Identified in Feral and Food Animals* (since 1981).

CHEMNAME (Columbus, OH: Chemical Abstracts Service). 1,300,000 substances, 1967–

This online chemical dictionary provides registry numbers, synonyms, molecular formulas, ring data, and other identifying information about all substances that have been cited at least twice in *Chemical Abstracts* since the beginning period of the eighth *Collective Index* in 1967.

CHEMSEARCH (Palo Alto, CA: DIALOG Information Services, Inc.). 95,000 substances, current

This nonbibliographic file contains dictionary-type information similar to that found in CHEMNAME for new substances reported recently in *Chemical Abstracts.* Substances already cited in CHEMNAME are not included here.

CHEMSIS (Palo Alto, CA: DIALOG Information Services, Inc.). 1,300,000 substances, 1967–

Substances which have been cited only once in *Chemical Abstracts* since 1967 are identified in this database. It provides registry numbers, formulas, synonyms, etc., for these rarely cited substances.

CHEMZERO (Palo Alto, CA: DIALOG Information Services, Inc.). 990,000 substances, current

Substances that have been registered by Chemical Abstracts Service but have not appeared in references covered by *Chemical Abstracts* since 1967 are identified in this dictionary file. Registry numbers and other information pertinent to the identification of these substances are provided.

Clinical Toxicology of Commercial Products (CTCP) (Washington, D.C.: Environmental Protection Agency and others). 20,000 records

Over 20,000 commercial, nonfood products available in the United States are described in terms of their chemical and toxicological effects. Corresponding to the printed tool of the same name, the database allows the user to search by manufacturer and trade name as well as by chemical names and CAS registry numbers of ingredients. Records provide data on toxic effects, symptoms, and recommended treatment.

COFFEELINE (London: International Coffee Organization). 9,500 citations, 1973–

Journal literature plus selected references from books, proceedings, and patents on all aspects of coffee production are indexed in this file. Agronomic, economic, and marketing topics are covered.

Comprehensive Dissertation Index (Ann Arbor, MI: University Microfilms, Inc.). 820,000 citations, 1861–

Virtually all American and a growing number of Canadian and other international doctoral dissertations are accessible through this database. Subject access is limited to the words appearing in the titles of the dissertations plus a descriptor for the department issuing the degree. For dissertations from institutions participating with University Microfilms for distribution of copies of the works, a reference to the abstract in *Dissertation Abstracts International* is part of the citation.

Current Research Information System (CRIS) (Washington, D.C.: U.S. Dept. of Agriculture, Cooperative State Research Service). 50,000 reports, current

The Current Research Information System (CRIS) is a nonbibliographic file containing brief descriptions of current research projects being conducted within the U.S. Department of Agriculture and the cooperating agricultural and forestry units in landgrant and forestry schools around the country. Reports for active projects and those that have been completed no more than two years are kept in the system. Records tend to be rather long in the database, and although there is a keyword bank that is used for indexing purposes, many of the records in the file do not have indexing terminology added to them. The user must, therefore, be particularly alert to possible terminological variations in the reports. There is a very high overlap in the areas of agricultural research between this database and the Smithsonian Science Information Exchange's SSIE Current Research database.

DRUGINFO (Minneapolis, MN: University of Minnesota, Drug Information Services). 12,000 citations, 1968–

Citations to books, journal articles, conference publications, and instructional materials in various media are contained in the DRUGINFO database. The scope of the file extends to the sociological and psychological aspects of drug use and drug abuse as well as to programs to educate drug users and the general public. Since 1980 the subject scope has been broadened to include alcohol use and abuse.

EIS: Environmental Impact Statements (Arlington, VA: Information Resources Press). 12,000 citations, 1970–

EIS provides highly structured abstracts of both draft and final environmental impact statements prepared for federal agencies under provisions of the National Environmental Policy Act. Subjects touched on in the reports include air and water quality, land use, and a host of topics related to physical, social, and aesthetic factors. In addition to general indexing, the database records allow for searching on specific aspects of the statements such as the positive or negative impacts and the alternatives considered to the proposed project.

ENVIROLINE (New York: Evironment Information Center, Inc.). 95,000 citations, 1971–

Multidisciplinary publications ranging from journals to government reports are indexed and abstracted for this file which provides comprehensive coverage of environmental research. In addition to technical literature on biological and chemical environmental issues, the database contains references to the social, economic, and legal dimensions of the topic. A code scheme that provides a rather broad-brush method of focusing search results is searchable in this file.

Environmental Bibliography (Santa Barbara, CA: Environmental Studies Institute). 225,000 citations, 1973–

This database contains references from over 300 periodicals covering human and animal nutrition and health, air and water quality, ecology, and environmental management. Subject access is limited to titles and keywords.

EPILEPSYLINE (Bethesda, MD: U.S. National Institutes of Health, Epilepsy Branch). 43,000 citations, 1945–

The database contains the references found in Section 50 of *Excerpta Medica,* known as *Epilepsy Abstracts,* plus additional references. Subjects covered include research, diagnosis, and treatment of seizures and convulsions. Records contain both substantial abstracts and descriptors drawn from the vocabulary tool used by *Excerpta Medica* entitled *Master List of Medical Terms* or *Malimet.*

Excerpta Medica (Amsterdam: Excerpta Medica). 2,200,000 citations, 1974–

The forty-three abstracting journals published by Excerpta Medica are merged and supplemented with more than 100,000 references each year to provide comprehensive coverage of biomedical research. Over 3,500 journals are abstracted. Particularly strong is the coverage of drug and pharmaceutical literature. Both extensive keywording and a code scheme are available to assist in refining retrieval.

Food Science and Technology Abstracts (Reading, England: International Food Information Service). 210,000 citations, 1969–

Over 1,200 journals along with selected books and patents provide international coverage of food technology and food sciences. Chemical, biochemical, and agricultural studies are included as well as other topics, such as engineering and economics. Abstracts and lengthy keyword indexing provide many access points to literature in this file; broad subject categories are available for searching on the file as it is made available by some online vendors. The file is British in origin, so the searcher must profile in such a way as to accommodate both British and American spelling and usage.

FOODS ADLIBRA (Louisville, KY: Komp Information Services, Inc.). 60,000 citations, 1974–

Over 250 publications, 500 technical journals, and patents from the United States and the United Kingdom are abstracted in this file. It provides coverage of developments in the food industry and of new food products. Nutrition and toxicology are also covered.

Forest Products (Madison, WI: Forest Products Research Society). 15,000 citations, 1947–

The database contains worldwide literature on wood and wood products from harvesting through manufacturing processes and marketing of finished goods. Coverage does not include chemical pulping nor the practice of forestry. Materials covered in addition to journal literature include patents, technical reports, conference publications, and government documents. Some overlap should be expected between this file and that of the Commonwealth Agricultural Bureaux (CAB), particularly for more recent literature.

Health Planning and Administration (Bethesda, MD: National Library of Medicine). 225,000 citations, 1975–

This composite index draws references from MEDLINE and from the printed *Hospital Literature Index.* Other health care journals are also scanned for items to be included in the file. Subject coverage is the non-clinical aspects of health care—management, planning, personnel, facilities, training, certification, and so forth.

International Pharmaceutical Abstracts (Bethesda, MD: American Society of Hospital Pharmacists). 75,000 citations, 1970–

Literature on research, development, use, and marketing of pharmaceuticals is abstracted from over 500 trade publications and medical and related journals. Particularly strong in this database is the information on study design.

IRL Life Science Collection (Bethesda, MD: Cambridge Scientific Abstracts). 375,000 citations, 1978–

Bibliographic citations from printed indexes such as *Animal Behavior Abstracts, Genetics Abstracts,* and *Microbiology Abstracts* are merged in this database (IRL—Information Retrieval Limited). Some fifteen such printed tools are contained in the file. Overlap will be heavy with databases such as TOXLINE, MEDLINE, CAB, and BIOSIS Previews. Database coverage is worldwide, incorporating references to journal and monographic publications.

ISI/BIOMED (Philadelphia, PA: Institute for Scientific Information). 750,000 citations, latest three years

Overlapping in its source citations with the SCISEARCH database in the areas of biomedicine, the ISI/BIOMED file provides more extensive searching of footnote references in the source articles appearing in some 1,300 major journals. The database introduces for online searching the capability of identifying sources that cite core literature—that is, the central papers of scientists working at the forefront of their research areas—in many hundred research specialties. This "research front" searching technique differs from ordinary cited-reference searching (also available on ISI/BIOMED) in that a preselection of leading authors in particular fields is made; so the user need not know all the key authors in the field in order to zero in on that core group of papers.

MEDLINE (Bethesda, MD: National Library of Medicine). 4,000,000 citations, 1966–

Worldwide clinical and biomedical journals and supporting literature in such fields as veterinary medicine, psychology, health planning and management, and education are indexed in this, the most authoritative general medical database. The file is created by the U. S. National Library of Medicine using the large, tightly controlled hierarchical thesaurus *Medical Subject Headings* (*MeSH*). Most major systems providing access to the file allow users to search both individual *MeSH* headings and larger hierarchical segments. Most MEDLINE searchers will find printed copies of the *MeSH* publications a necessity for successful results. Since the mid-1970s abstracts appearing in source journals have been made a part of the database records, so that now about half of the newer records have summaries in the file.

National Technical Information Service (NTIS) (Springfield, VA: National Technical Information Service). 1,000,000 citations, 1964– (some materials to the mid-1950s)

This interdisciplinary database consists of citations to technical reports resulting from the work of federal government agencies and their contractors. All fields are represented in the file, but heaviest emphasis is in areas of pure and applied sciences. Substantial environmental, agricultural, and biomedical research is covered by the reports in the database. Vocabulary control in the file is achieved through a variety of thesauri including the *Thesaurus of Engineering and Scientific Terms* and the *Thesaurus of Water Resources Terms.*

Oceanic Abstracts (Bethesda, MD: Cambridge Scientific Abstracts). 125,000 citations, 1964–

Physical, chemical, and biological research of the ocean environment and information on economic and social aspects of maritime activities are included in this file. Materials are abstracted from journals, reports, government publications, and conference proceedings. Indexing includes both general subject terms and terminology to facilitate searching for specifically named organisms. Coverage is worldwide.

Pharmaceutical News Index (Louisville, KY: Data Courier, Inc.). 80,000 citations, 1975–

Current developments in the fields of pharmaceuticals, cosmetics, and related medical fields are included from leading trade news publications such as the *FDC Reports* ("The Pink Sheet"), *Drug Research Reports* ("The Blue Sheet"), etc.

Registry of Toxic Effects of Chemical Substances (RTECS) (Cincinnati, OH: U. S. National Institutes of Health, National Institute for Occupational Safety and Health). 50,000 citations, 1971–

This factual database contains identifying information and data on the toxicity of some 50,000 substances registered under provisions of the Toxic Substances Control Act (TSCA). Records in the file provide identification through Chemical Abstracts Service name, CAS registry number and synonyms, molecular formula, and Wiswesser Line Notation. Toxicity data contained in the file may include, among other data elements, *in vivo* measures, both chronic and acute; *in vitro* mutagenicity; eye and skin irritation; particular toxic effects, such as carcinogenesis; and threshold limits.

SCISEARCH (Philadelphia, PA: Institute for Scientific Information). 4,500,000 citations, 1970–

All editorial matter from nearly 3,000 of the most important scientific and technical journals is indexed in this multidisciplinary database. Coverage includes not only articles but also letters, reviews, correction notices, and editorials. All footnotes are indexed so that a searcher can identify new literature through its association, via footnote citations, to older significant works. All fields of science are covered. Subject access is restricted to words appearing in titles of articles, so profiles for subject searches in this database need to be particularly flexible in order to allow retrieval from many variant words and word combinations.

SSIE Current Research (Springfield, VA: National Technical Information Service). 175,000 reports, current

Project descriptions of research activities funded by federal, state, and some private sources make up this multidisciplinary file produced by the Smithsonian Science Information Exchange. The text of the descriptions and an extensive list of indexing terms makes information in this file particularly accessible. All fields of inquiry are covered, with special strength in science and technology. Somewhat modified project descriptions from the U. S. Department of Agriculture's Current Research Information System database CRIS are included in this file, so the overlap between SSIE and CRIS online will be quite high in areas of agricultural research.

Superindex (Boca Raton, FL: Superindex, Inc.). 2,000,000 citations, 1967–

This database is composed of the indexes created from some 600 major scientific, technical, and professional reference works such as the publications of Chemical Rubber Company Press, the American Society for Testing and Materials, and Springer-Verlag. Available through this database are citations to formulas, tables, and specific pieces of information appearing in these reference works.

TELEGEN (New York: Environment Information Center, Inc.). 6,500 citations, 1973–

International sources of information on the emerging fields associated with genetic engineering are covered in this database. Corresponding to the printed *Telegen Reports,* this file covers books, proceedings, reports, government publications, and journal literature.

TOXLINE (Bethesda, MD: National Library of Medicine, Toxicology Information Center). 1,400,000 citations, 1965– (selectively to 1940)

Toxicological literature drawn from *Index Medicus, Chemical Abstracts,* and *Biological Abstracts* is merged into this database. Indexing terminology from the National Library of Medicine's publication, *Medical Subject Headings* (*MeSH*) plus additional uncontrolled keywords and other tags such as CAS registry numbers are added to the online records to improve retrievability of information. Most citations contain abstracts of up to 200 words. The scope of the database includes both analytical studies of chemical substances and clinical studies of their effects on organisms.

TROPAG (Amsterdam, Royal Tropical Institute). 32,300 citations, 1975–

The machine-readable version of *Abstracts of Tropical Agriculture,* this database provides worldwide coverage of agricultural research and practice in tropical and subtropical areas. Agronomy, soil science, animal husbandry, as well as economic and social research relevant to the agricultural situation in these regions of the world are included in the file.

Water Resources Abstracts (Washington, D.C.: U.S. Dept. of the Interior, Water Resources Information Center). 145,000 citations, 1968–

The machine-readable equivalent of the U. S. Department of the Interior's *Selected Water Resources Abstracts,* this database provides access to journal, report, and monographic literature. All aspects of water-resources research and management are included, from economics and planning to water quality and the biology of aquatic environments. Most citations contain substantial abstracts. Indexing terminology is derived from the *Thesaurus of Water Resources Terms,* also published by the U.S. Department of the Interior.

World Textiles (Manchester, England: Shirley Institute). 120,000 citations, 1970–

Scientific research on textiles and fibers plus technical literature on the economics and technology of the textile industry are covered in this file. Scope of the database is international and includes journals, proceedings, patents, reports, and standards.

Zoological Record (Philadelphia, PA: BioSciences Information Services and the Zoological Society of London). 75,000 citations, 1978–

With heavy emphasis on systematics and taxonomy, this database covers the international literature of zoology. All animals are covered, from protozoans to mammals, as they are reported on in some 6,000 journals. Effective use of this file will require the consultation of standard zoological nomenclature publications.

4
Social Sciences and Education

Characteristics and Terminology

The conditions and phenomena that concern both social scientists and practitioners of human service professions touch virtually every aspect of the world as we know it. From the anthropologist who is called in to investigate artifacts unearthed during a construction project or a psychologist investigating perceptual problems associated with highway safety to an academic dean trying to establish a form of governance for his college, the social sciences provide many rich avenues for investigation. Because the routes of inquiry are so varied, the literature of the social sciences is likely to be dispersed, a situation offering many challenges to library research projects.

Although some sources define social sciences to include business disciplines and law, here, these three fields will be covered in separate chapters. Emphasis in this chapter will be on the disciplines of anthropology, education, political science, history, psychology, sociology, economics, geography, and information science. In establishing these limits, however, one must realize that true boundaries rarely exist in the social science field. The categories, such as anthropology and sociology, may be better characterized as sharing zones of mutual concern than as having clear lines of demarcation, and this lack of clear divisions can also be found between some of the social sciences and some of the disciplines in the physical and life sciences. It is sometimes difficult, for example, to decide where the work of the psychologist ends and that of the brain physiologist begins when both choose to focus on the organic basis of sensation. The situation is further complicated for practitioners in the social sciences—government officials, policy makers, personnel administrators, etc.—by the interdisciplinary nature of human and organizational problems.

The administrator who chooses to undertake a major reorganization of a department must realize that there are both sociological and psychological factors that must be dealt with if such a venture is to be successful. For example, what will be the psychological impact on workers who are to be integrated into newly created units with new supervisors? What happens to the performance of former supervisors who will lose some of their authority because of reorganization? What effect will the reorganization have on lines of communication within the organization as a whole? These problems plus a multitude of similar ones are intermixed and do not lend themselves easily to disentanglement.

The problem is not always merely one of several social sciences interacting either, for there are major social science considerations important in technological fields as well. Ergonomics, or human factors engineering—to take but an obvious example—plays an important role in the design of devices and products as diverse as jet aircraft display panels, assembly line work stations, and signage systems for a large hospital.

The eclectic nature of social science research produces for the student and scholar a morass of terminology, much of it consisting of common words and phrases to which has been applied special meaning. Words such as "termination," "stress," or "value" have a generally understood meaning in normal discourse, but they also have more specialized meanings in fields such as administration or psychology. Computers are very efficient at identifying terms such as these, but they have little ability in determining whether the words are being used in the sense desired by the reader. To illustrate, a literature search for articles on stress management may very well turn up citations with sentences similar to this one: "Managing a kindergarten classroom is a task that stresses good organization and a sense of adventure." The clues to relevance in a reference such as this one are wholly contextual, which makes profiling for highly relevant initial bibliographies a treacherous and frustrating undertaking.

Many concerns of the social scientist are intangible. He or she is describing phenomena and behaviors that have simultaneous existences in any of several theoretical constructs all of which are "correct," depending on the perceptions or needs of the researcher. Unlike lithium compounds or individual species of orchids, there is seldom a commonly recognized set of naming conventions that can be used to identify new social science phenomena. As a result a phenomenon or set of behaviors is, in a sense, what the observer says it is. If that phenomenon is observed and studied over a long enough period of time, a consensus usually evolves about what it will be called, but that process usually takes several years. In the meantime, searches through published literature become games of semantic and syntactic chess.

Akin to the general problem of simply naming conditions and phenomena in the social sciences is the problem of labeling, particularly as it relates to human conditions. Words have power both to aid understanding and to help effect change. Consequently, social scientists are particularly atuned to the terms used to label people and their situations. To some degree the labels in use today reflect both changes in general societal attitudes and greater understanding of conditions as a result of research. To offer but one illustration, consider the labels that may have been applied to a ten-year-old boy who, although physically normal, can read only at first-grade level. In the early part of this century he might have been called feeble-minded; later he might have been considered mentally retarded. As understanding of learning processes have grown, he may very well today be classified as learning disabled or perhaps dyslexic. These labels are applied carefully in professional psychological and counseling literature, but the level of precision with which they are used in other fields such as political science or sociology cannot be predicted. These variations in the use of terms will increase the problems in doing a thorough literature review since relevant citations may appear under a number of headings.

Finally, even a cursory glance through the literature in most social science disciplines reveals a dismaying number of allusive or "literary" titles, those titles using words that "grab" the reader. "You Gotta Kiss a Lotta Frogs before You Find Prince Charming" may arrest the eye of the reader of *English Journal* and cause him to read the article, but there is nothing there to help the search analyst insure that that item will be retrieved in a search of the ERIC database on the topic of reading habits among secondary school students. Producers of most social science databases, in recognition of this problem, assign keywords and/or write abstracts that more accurately describe the contents of references, so usually the keywords or phrases in the abstract will insure retrieval. Such titles, however, frequently creep into other searches because of the unusual language in their titles. For example, the title just mentioned might also be retrieved in a search on laboratory curricula for high school biology courses where frog dissection was featured.

Profiling Assistance

Terminological pitfalls dot the social science landscape, but there are a number of tools and search techniques that can make online searches of these fields easier and more productive. In fields where appropriate keywords may not be readily apparent, starting the search process with one or two recent papers known to be relevant to the topic will often prove valuable. If copies of such works are available, they can assist directly in the profiling process by suggesting words and phrases. If the articles are not available for inspection or if they do not provide adequate search terms, these titles can be called up online in an appropriate database. By displaying their keyword phrases one is able to see how items known to be relevant were indexed; then other citations indexed similarly can be retrieved by using these keywords.

Thesauri

There are several thesauri available for use in profile construction. Although each thesaurus was developed for a specific field, such as political science or education, the overlap in social science disciplines frequently makes a thesaurus developed for one discipline a useful profiling tool for another. One must keep in mind, of course, that the terms found in a thesaurus may well need to be supplemented by other terms, especially if the thesaurus is being used for profile construction in a collateral field.

Although thesaurus formats vary widely, one of the most commonly used arrangements can be illustrated by the sample entry from the *Thesaurus of ERIC Descriptors* (Figure 4-1), which

FACTOR ANALYSIS *Jul. 1966*
CIJE: 1,382 RIE: 1,120 GC: 820
SN Mathematical methods used to explain the relationships observed among a large number of descriptive variables in terms of a smaller number of underlying or inferred factors
UF Centroid Method Of Factor Analysis
Maximum Likelihood Factor Analysis #
Principal Components Analysis
NT Oblique Rotation
Orthogonal Rotation
BT Multivariate Analysis
RT Ability Identification
Cluster Analysis
Correlation
Discriminant Analysis
Factor Structure
Goodness Of Fit
Item Analysis
Least Squares Statistics
Maximum Likelihood Statistics
Multidimensional Scaling
Path Analysis
Personality Assessment
Q Methodology
Research Methodology
Test Construction
Testing
Test Validity
Transformations (Mathematics)
Trend Analysis

Figure 4-1. Entry from Thesaurus of ERIC Descriptors.

is the vocabulary control tool for several bibliographic tools in the field of education. The entry for "Factor Analysis" contains the date that that term was first used to index items in the ERIC system. That system began in 1966; so a term with a creation date later than 1966 should be a clue to the search strategist that other, less standard, terms probably were in use prior to that time and that additional terms will be needed for a thorough search of the literature. The RIE/CIJE postings notes indicate how many documents have had the term "Factor Analysis" assigned to them in *Resources in Education* and *Current Index to Journals in Education,* two of the primary indexing publications of the ERIC system. High postings—or document counts—would indicate the need for additional search qualifiers in order to narrow results to a manageable size. Low postings would be an indication that supplementary terms may be needed to identify all relevant items in the database.

The *Scope Note* (SN) may contain a brief explanation of how indexers are to understand a particular term and/or a statement to the database user about how the term has been used in the past. Such notes can be of inestimable value when searching in areas where similar sounding terms are used to index quite different ideas.

Following the scope note can be found an array of terminology grouped under any of four major categories. UF indicates those terms that the descriptor is *Used For,* that is, the nonindex terms for which the descriptor is considered equivalent. In a system using the *Thesaurus of ERIC Descriptors* the term "Employment Patterns," for example, would be preferred to the terms "Employment Trends" and "Job Holding Patterns." The searcher may find those terms very useful, however, in constructing a search of *Sociological Abstracts* or the *Social Sciences Citation Index.* NT, or *Narrower Terms,* designate those other authorized keywords that are considered to denote a narrower aspect of the term being looked at. BT, or *Broader Terms,* are those authorized keywords considered broader in their definition or scope than the term looked up. RT denotes *Related Terms,* those descriptors that bear some logical relation to a descriptor but are not so closely related as to be narrower or broader terms.

Not every thesaurus has every one of these features, and indeed, not every entry in the ERIC thesaurus has all the elements displayed here. Most thesauri, however, exhibit terminology in a manner analogous to the illustration. They may in addition provide the user with other conceptual groupings of terms. For example, Figure 4-2 illustrates a portion of a categorized display in the *Political Science Thesaurus.* Such listings can be of particular help when one has difficulty in determining even the proper terms to begin a search of the main thesaurus or when one is looking for a particular constellation of terms that are allied with each other but bear no hierarchical relationship.

S-11 CULTURE TYPE

S-11-0001	1975	00007	Culture Type
S-11-0002	1979	00000	.Civilization
S-11-0003	1979	00000	..African Civilization
S-11-0004	1979	00000	..Ancient Civilization
S-11-0005	1979	00000	..Byzantine Civilization
S-11-0006	1979	00000	..Eastern Civilization
S-11-0007	1979	00000	..Greek Civilization
S-11-0008	1979	00000	..Islamic Civilization
S-11-0009	1979	00000	..Roman Civilization
S-11-0010	1979	00000	..Western Civilization
S-11-0011	1975	00014	.Community Culture
S-11-0012	1975	00012	..Village Culture
S-11-0013	1975	00011	.Counter Culture
S-11-0014	1975	00010	.Drug Culture
S-11-0015	1975	00043	.Ethnic Culture
S-11-0016	1975	00014	..Black Culture
S-11-0017	1975	00007	.Heterogeneous Culture
S-11-0018	1975	00004	.Homogeneous Culture
S-11-0019	1979	00000	.Mass Culture
S-11-0020	1979	00000	..Popular Culture
S-11-0021	1975	00009	.Nonwestern Culture
S-11-0022	1975	00019	..Eastern Culture
S-11-0023	1975	00055	.Political Culture
S-11-0024	1975	00003	..Modern Political Culture
S-11-0025	1975	00002	...Political Professionalization
S-11-0026	1975	00001	...Political Secularization
S-11-0027	1975	00014	..National Political Culture
S-11-0028	1975	00007	...Civic Culture
S-11-0029	1975	00000	....Legalistic Political Culture
S-11-0030	1979	00000	....Parochial Political Culture
S-11-0031	1975	00003	....Pragmatic Political Culture
S-11-0032	1975	00002	....Secular Political Culture
S-11-0033	1975	00002	....Subject Participant Culture
S-11-0034	1975	00007	....Traditional Political Culture

Figure 4-2. Entry from Political Science Thesaurus categorized display.

Among the many thesauri available in the social sciences the five listed here are among the most useful for profile construction in a broad range of social science subdisciplines.

- *Thesaurus of ERIC Descriptors,* revised ed. (Phoenix, AZ.: Oryx Press, 1980). A 419-page listing of over 6,700 terms used in all disciplines related to educational administration and practice. In addition to the curriculum-related fields, one will find represented terms appropriate to psychology, sociology, linguistics, applied statistics, information science, and public administration. It is the vocabularly authority for databases such as ERIC, Exceptional Child Education Resources, and Resources in Vocational Education.

- *Political Science Thesaurus II,* 2nd ed. by Carl Beck, Thomas McKechnie, and Paul Evan Peters (Washington, D.C.: American Political Science Association, 1979). Developed to serve as the vocabulary authority for the indexing service and database *U.S. Political Science Documentation,* this thesaurus provides a useful guide to terminology not only in political science but also in sociology, urban planning, social psychology, management, and areas of philosophy.

- *Thesaurus of Psychological Index Terms,* 3rd ed. (Washington, D.C.: American Psychological Association, 1982). This 258-page volume provides guidance to terms in behavioral, clinical, educational, social, experimental, and applied psychology.

- *Thesaurus of Engineering and Scientific Terms* (New York: Engineer's Joint Council, 1967). Developed to provide terminological authority for information tools such as that of the National Technical Information Service, this thesaurus is heavily weighted toward concepts, apparatus, and processes in the hard sciences and engineering. It does, however, provide scores of entries in social science disciplines, particularly political science, administration, social psychology, sociology, and planning.

- *Library of Congress Subject Headings,* 9th ed. (with supplements) (Washington, D.C., 1980). This enormous reference work is the subject authority for catalogers in most academic and research libraries in the United States. All fields of knowledge are covered with abundant cross references. It does, however, tend to be somewhat slower than more subject-specific vocabulary tools in updating its terminology.

Other Printed Aids

Thesauri can be invaluable in finding appropriate synonyms for a search profile, but they are not available for every database. Annual cumulative subject indexes and subject-oriented dictionaries or encyclopedias can fill this gap for many files. By consulting cumulative volumes for indexes such as the *Public Affairs Information Service Bulletin* or *America: History and Life,* the user can find specific subject headings and related cross references used by database indexers. By scanning a few specific entries under relevant major headings, he may also be able to discern common word variations that will improve the quality of his search. Subject indexes for a tool such as *Sociological Abstracts* may also alert users to possible word variations or commonly used abbreviations. For example, the entry in a recent issue of that index for "innovation" appeared as "innovation -s, -ive, -iveness, -or, -ors"—indicating that all those forms of that term may be encountered in the database. A search on the stem "innovat-," therefore, would be appropriate for a computer search.

Dictionaries and encylcopedic works devoted to specific disciplines can frequently prove useful for generating lists of search terms. While most appropriate for legal research, tools such as *Corpus Juris Secundum* or *Black's Law Dictionary* can also help in concept development for searches in business, political science, planning, and other policy-oriented fields. Works such as the multi-volume *International Encyclopedia of the Social Sciences* or Greenwald's *Encyclopedia of Economics* cover fundamental concepts in social science disciplines. Perusal of the text, the bibliographies, and especially the lengthy indexes will often reveal numerous useful search terms.

Classification Schemes

Systems for categorizing and classifying have captured people's imaginations throughout history. All such schemes are ultimately arbitrary, but in the disciplines of the natural sciences, at least, there has developed over recent history widespread acceptance of particular classification schemes such as the periodic table in chemistry or the major taxonomic structures for plants and animals. To be sure, none of these systems has proved to be immutable, and although there may be revision of parts of the scheme from time to time, there remains a general acceptance and understanding of the basic conceptual framework.

In the social sciences, however, such classification schemes do not fare so well. There is rarely any "natural" relationship that would provide the basis for classification, no obvious, quantifiable progression from simpler forms to more complex forms. Indeed some of the most hotly debated issues in social science literature deal precisely with issues arising from attempts to classify social science phenomena. The indexing and abstracting services covering these disciplines have been no more successful in such efforts to categorize the field than have the scholars. There is, however, some measure of assistance for the computer searcher in the coding schemes available in some databases. In instances where the online database allows searching by section heading, the user can often improve the focus of the search results to some degree. Usually the section headings in a database correspond to major sections of the printed tool from which the database derives. Rarely are social science databases divided as finely as are scientific files such as *Chemical Abstracts* or *Biological Abstracts,* yet the section codes can help put search terms into a narrower context that can help the user. In databases where a particular section heading fits closely the limits of one concept in the proposed search strategy, the user may be able to use it as a shorthand method of entering that concept. A user, for instance, who wants to review the recent literature on the psychological effect job loss has on family relationships might effectively use the *Psychological Abstracts* section-heading code for "Marriage and Family," in place of, or as a supplement to, a list of words and phrases denoting that aspect of the search.

Of course, not every database contains those codes, and those that do may not divide the literature in a way that will make the codes useful for every potential question. Three of the code schemes that may be useful are described here.

- *Psychological Abstracts.* In printed form *Psychological Abstracts* is divided into sixteen major categories ranging from "General Psychology" to "Physiological Intervention" and "Educational Psychology." From 1967 through 1975 the large headings were not more finely divided. Beginning in 1976, however, numerous subcategories were created, so for the recent years, a user can focus more precisely on topics such as "Language and Speech" or "Literature and Art" as narrower aspects of communication psychology. A complete list of the headings can be found in the *Thesaurus of Psychological Index Terms,* 3rd ed.
- *COSATI Codes.* The Committee on Scientific and Technical Information devised a classification scheme used by the National Technical Information Service (NTIS) in its publications (now combined into one and called *Government Reports Announcements and Index*). The view is rather broad (e.g. "05A—Administration and Management" or "15G—Military Operations, Strategy, and Tactics"), but even this broad classification can prove to be invaluable in eliminating irrelevancies in a database as large and eclectic in its subject coverage as NTIS. Thus, a political science professor doing research on the community's role in cable television might use the COSATI field designators 05A "Administration and Management" and 05D "History, Law, and Political Science" in order to focus a word search on "cable television" or "community access television" to only those items dealing with policy or societal issues.
- *Sociological Abstracts.* Section-heading codes in the Sociological Abstracts database correspond to the major parts of the printed tool. The breakdown is rather broad, but some level of improvement in precision of search results should be possible with their use. For example, by using the section-heading code equivalent to "Sociology of Medicine" in

conjunction with terms such as "Mexican American," "Hispanic," and "Chicano," a search strategy can identify efficiently pertinent references on the topic of the sociological aspects of health care among Spanish-speaking groups in the United States.

The help that these thesauri and other search aids can provide will depend to a large degree on the topic being searched. In instances where consensus has emerged quickly regarding terminology, search results will very likely be highly relevant. More likely, however, will be the situation in which the search strategist will need to build concepts to encompass a fairly broad range of synonyms, antonyms, and variant word forms. When this sort of strategy is used, the user of the resulting bibliography may also find larger and less precise printouts necessary in order to be assured that the highest number of truly relevant papers have been retrieved. But most researchers would have to agree that editing a working bibliography of a hundred potentially relevant references printed out from a computer search is much easier than searching manually through dozens of volumes of the corresponding printed indexes.

Databases

The databases listed here are the files dealing almost exclusively with social science topics with the exception of business and law, which are treated in separate chapters. The researcher needs to remember that many other databases will contain sizable numbers of social science references as well. The DOE Energy Data Base (Chapter 5), for example, covers all aspects of energy, including hundreds of papers on energy policymaking, sociological aspects of energy shortages, education for energy conservation, and so forth.

AIM/ARM (Columbus, OH: The National Center for Research in Vocational Education). 17,500 citations, 1967–1976

Nonjournal literature on vocational-technical education can be tapped with this database. Abstracts of instructional materials and research reports from school districts, government departments, and industrial organizations are included. Indexing terms were drawn from the *Thesaurus of ERIC Descriptors.* This file is now closed; the new materials on vocational-technical education have been added to the ERIC database and to the new database called Resources in Vocational Education (RIVE).

America: History and Life (AHL) (Santa Barbara, CA: ABC-CLIO, Inc.). 175,000 citations, 1964–

Articles, books, and dissertations on all areas of history in the United States and Canada are abstracted for the AHL database. Political, social, and economic history as well as area studies, historiography, and popular culture are among the areas covered. In addition to abstracts and indexing terminology, the database provides tagging for historical periods covered in the items indexed for the file.

American Statistics Index (Bethesda, MD: Congressional Information Service, Inc.). 90,000 citations, 1973–

This database indexes and abstracts the statistical publications of the United States government. Both recurring reports of a statistical nature and more comprehensive, one-time compilations are covered. Greatest emphasis is on those publications containing social, economic, demographic, and natural resources data, but some scientific and technical publications are included as well. Information can be retrieved on the basis of general subjects as well as by an array of specific characteristics of the data itself. For example, it is possible to specify that only publications with data reported by county or by occupation be retrieved.

Bilingual Education Bibliographic Abstracts (Rosslyn, VA: National Clearinghouse for Bilingual Education). 5,000 citations, 1978–

The educational and cultural dimensions of bilingualism are covered in this file, created by the National Clearinghouse for Bilingual Education. Records in the file range from journal articles and published reviews, to classroom materials, reports, and manuscripts. Indexing terms, drawn from the *Thesaurus of ERIC Descriptors,* and abstracts of up to about 200 words aid subject retrieval. Topics covered include linguistics, second-language teaching, curriculum development, and culture related to learning in a bilingual setting.

BLS Consumer Price Index (Washington, D.C.: U.S. Dept. of Labor, Bureau of Labor Statistics, Division of Consumer Prices and Price Indexes). 9,000 records, varying dates

The U. S. Bureau of Labor Statistics' indexes of consumer prices for various geographic areas and population segments are searchable in this file. The data available in the file are presented tabularly.

BLS Employment, Hours, and Earnings (Washington, D.C.: U.S. Dept. of Labor, Bureau of Labor Statistics). 25,000 records, varying dates

Time series data on employment, hours of work, and earnings in various industries of the United States are covered in this file. Up to twenty years of annual data and ten years of quarterly data are included, broken down by numerous categories such as Standard Metropolitan Statistical Area (SMSA), sex, industry, or type of worker. Information retrievable is numeric rather than narrative.

BLS Labor Force (Washington, D.C.: U.S. Dept. of Labor, Bureau of Labor Statistics). 15,000 records, varying dates

Broken down by various demographic, social, and economic delimiters, this database provides access to time series data on the U.S. employment situation. Data on employment, unemployment, and nonparticipation in the labor force are covered. Up to twenty years of annual data and ten years of quarterly data are available in many of the series contained in the file.

BLS Producer Price Index (Washington, D.C.: U.S. Dept. of Labor, Bureau of Labor Statistics). 7,000 records, varying dates

Wholesale price indexes for over 2,800 commodities are contained in this file from the U. S. Bureau of Labor Statistics. Up to twenty years of annual data and ten years of quarterly data are provided in many of the series.

Canadian Newspaper Index (Toronto, Canada: Micromedia Ltd.). 320,000 citations, 1977–

All textual matter from seven leading Canadian newspapers is indexed in this file. Included in the file are the following: *Montreal Star, Toronto Globe and Mail, Toronto Star, Vancouver Sun, Winnipeg Free Press, Calgary Herald,* and *Halifax Chronicle-Herald.*

Catalyst Resources for Women (New York: Catalyst Library). 3,000 citations, 1963–

Women in the workforce is the focus of this database, which contains bibliographic citations to articles, books, government reports, and other publications. All aspects of the working life of women are covered, including information on career education and planning, two-career families, and personnel practices of individual companies.

Child Abuse and Neglect (Washington, D.C.: U. S. Dept. of Health and Human Services, National Center on Child Abuse and Neglect). 13,000 citations, 1965–

Professional and research materials touching all areas of child abuse and neglect are indexed in this file. Materials covered include bibliographic references, descriptions of current research projects, descriptions of ongoing programs and projects, legal citations, and audiovisual materials. Only English language materials are included, and research projects and ongoing programs are limited to those in the United States.

Comprehensive Dissertation Index (Ann Arbor, MI: University Microfilms International, Inc.). 820,000 citations, 1861–

Virtually all American and a growing number of Canadian and international doctoral dissertations are accessible through this database. Subject access is limited to the words appearing in the titles of the dissertations plus a descriptor for the department issuing the degree. Citations to *Dissertation Abstracts International* are a part of the database record where that is available.

Congressional Information Service (Bethesda, MD: Congressional Information Service). 170,000 citations, 1970–

This database contains references to the working papers of the Congress, the hearings and the staff papers of U.S. House of Representatives and Senate committees. Indexing is very detailed, down to the testimony of individual witnesses. This is the machine-readable version of the *Index to Publications of the United States Congress.*

Congressional Record Abstracts (Washington, D.C.: Capitol Services, Inc.). 225,000 citations, 1976–

A comprehensive index to each issue of the *Congressional Record,* this file provides access to the bills, resolutions, reports, speeches, and inserted items from members of the U.S. Congress. In addition, the database provides coverage of floor debates and roll call votes. Indexing structure and abstracts increase the accessibility of information in this database.

CRECORD (Washington, D.C.: Capitol Services, Inc.). 250,000 citations, 1976–

The file contains detailed indexing of the *Congressional Record,* including not only the House and Senate journals, Extension of Remarks, and the Digest sections, but also references to bills, resolutions, reports, and committee actions. Coverage extends from the beginning of the second session of the 94th Congress.

Criminal Justice Periodicals Index (Ann Arbor, MI: University Microfilms International, Inc.). 90,000 citations, 1975–

Research and professional level literature from some 120 journals is contained in this database which includes subject coverage on topics such as juvenile delinquency, law enforcement, drug abuse, penology, white collar crime, and other related topics.

Deadline Data on World Affairs. (Parsippany, NJ: New York Times Information Service, Inc.). Records for over 250 entities, current

A machine-readable version of the long standard reference card file, this database provides current information on the political, social, economic and demographic facts of the countries of the world and all states and provinces of the United States and Canada. In addition to selected bibliographic citations, the file also provides factual data and some statistics.

Economics Abstracts International (Oxford, England: Learned Information, Ltd.). 115,000 citations, 1974–

The computerized equivalent to the printed *Economic Titles/Abstracts* and *Key to Economic Science and Management Science,* this database covers the world's economy as reported in some 1,800 journal and monographic sources. The file contains information on markets, finance, industries, trade, and the economies of specific countries and regions of the world.

ERIC (Bethesda, MD: U.S. Dept. of Education, National Institute of Education). 500,000 citations, 1966–

Comprehensive coverage of journal literature and monographic literature in all areas of educational theory and practice is provided in this database, which is the equivalent of *Current Index to Journals in Education* (CIJE) and *Resources in Education* (RIE). Over 700 journals and many thousands of additional reports, addresses, curriculum materials, and other publications are scanned for inclusion in the file by the staff of the clearinghouses of the Educational Resources Information Center, a federal information agency. Subject scope encompasses all areas of potential value to education professionals, from curriculum development and classroom management to school administration and counseling psychology. Indexing terminology is controlled through the *Thesaurus of ERIC Descriptors,* a necessary search aid for effective and efficient use of the file. Annotations for journal citations and substantial professionally written abstracts for other documents increase the retrievability of citations from the database.

Exceptional Child Education Resources (Reston, VA: The Council for Exceptional Children). 50,000 citations, 1966–

Although overlapping by as much as 50 percent the materials in the ERIC database, this file can prove a valuable resource for research- and professional-level information on the education of children with exceptional needs, either through their giftedness or through some physical, mental, or emotional handicap. Journal literature as well as published and unpublished materials are referenced in the file which, in subject matter, includes curriculum materials, guidelines, descriptions of programs, and research conducted in all areas of educational practice. Indexing is controlled by the *Thesaurus of ERIC Descriptors.*

Family Resources Database (Minneapolis, MN: National Council on Family Relations, Family Resource and Referral Center). 50,000 citations, 1970–

The entire range of materials from journal articles and books to teaching aids and audiovisuals are indexed in this database which provides comprehensive coverage of family-related research and professional practice. Subject matter includes sociological, economic, psychological, legal, and political dimensions of the field. Records contain abstracts and indexing terms drawn from the National Council on Family Relation's *Thesaurus of Marriage and Family.*

Federal Energy Data Index (FEDEX) (Washington, D.C.: U.S. Dept. of Energy, National Energy Information Center). 2,500 citations, 1977–

Indexing both the separate publications of the Energy Information Administration (EIA) and selected graphs and statistical tables within those publications, FEDEX provides rather detailed access to federal statistics on energy—its production, consumption, and costs.

GPO Monthly Catalog (Washington, D.C.: U.S. Government Printing Office). 175,000 citations, 1976–

This database corresponds to the publication *Monthly Catalog of United States Government Publications.* In it users will find reports, handbooks, technical manuals, statistical compilations, maps, and a wide variety of other publications on the entire range of subjects in which the federal government has an interest. For social scientists the database will be a rich resource, particularly for administration, educational policy, and legislative processes. No abstracts are provided in the database, but subject indexing is relatively thorough, providing improved access to fairly narrow topics.

HISTLINE (Bethesda, MD: National Library of Medicine, History of Medicine Program). 60,000 citations, 1970–

Corresponding to the National Library of Medicine's *Bibliography of the History of Medicine,* this file contains citations to articles, books, and conference papers on the history of medicine, the medical profession, medical technique and technology, and medical institutions. In addition, the database contains many references on the history of diseases, drugs and medicinal plants, folk medicine, and other related fields.

Historical Abstracts. (Santa Barbara, CA: ABC-CLIO, Inc.). 125,000 citations, 1973–

Over 2,000 journals in history and related disciplines are scanned for information relating to social, economic, political, and military history. Scope of the file is defined as world history (excluding the United States and Canada) from 1450 to the present. Indexing terms, data designators for historical periods, and brief abstracts will aid retrieval from the file. Coverage of source materials is worldwide, so a sizable portion of the references will be in non–English language publications.

Instructional Resources Information System (IRIS) (Columbus, OH: U.S. Environmental Protection Agency, Instructional Resources Center). 4,000 citations, 1979–

A comprehensive file of instructional materials in all media for education and training in the field of water resources, this database covers topics such as water quality, waste disposal, water resource management, and collateral fields such as pesticides and toxicology.

Journal of Economic Literature (Nashville, TN: American Economic Association). 100,000 citations, 1969–

Over 250 economics journals and some 200 monographs are indexed annually in this database, corresponding to the printed *Index of Economic Articles* and the *Journal of Economic Literature.* All aspects of economic theory and research are included, from macro-economic studies, to articles on individual commodities and industries. In addition to title words and keywords, the file makes available the rather detailed numeric classification scheme used in the printed equivalents.

LC/LINE. See MACHINE READABLE CATALOGING (MARC)

LC MARC. See MACHINE READABLE CATALOGING (MARC)

LIBRARY AND INFORMATION SCIENCE ABSTRACTS (LISA) (London: The Library Association). 45,000 citations, 1969–

Books, reports, and other monographic publications plus over 300 journals are covered in this database which provides access to professional literature in library science, library management, information science, and the technologies that support these fields. Scope of the database is international. The file is created by the Library Association of the U. K., so profiles on this database will need to accommodate British spelling and usage.

Machine Readable Cataloging (MARC) (Washington, D.C.: Library of Congress). 1,000,000 citations, 1968–

This file contains complete bibliographic records from the Machine Readable Cataloging (MARC) program of the Library of Congress. Some versions of this database are also known as LC/LINE and LC MARC. English language materials since 1968 and non-English materials from varying dates since that time are included. The file can be searched by author, title, and subject as well as by a number of other access points such as imprint date and publisher. All subject fields are represented, but the file should be of particular value to researchers in book-related disciplines such as the humanities and the social sciences.

Magazine Index (Menlo Park, CA: Information Access Co.). 1,330,000 citations, 1959–

This database is a broadly based general reference file covering nearly 400 general interest periodicals such as *Time* and *Harper's*. Popular-level coverage in all fields is provided, and the file is particularly suited to inquiries in the areas of popular culture, public affairs, and current events. Indexing terminology is based on *Library of Congress Subject Headings* and supplemented for new concepts, proper names, and specific products.

Mental Health Abstracts (Bethesda, MD: U.S. Alcohol, Drug Abuse, and Mental Health Administration, National Institute of Mental Health). 375,000 citations, 1969–

Covering worldwide journal and monographic literature, this database provides access to literature on all aspects of mental health. Both clinical and experimental literature is included. The database serves as the source for several specific print tools such as *Psychopharmacology Abstracts* or *Bibliography on Racism;* there is not, however, a print equivalent to the entire file. Substantial overlap with the PSYCHINFO database can be expected.

Monitor (Wooster, OH: Bell and Howell). 7,500 citations, 1979–

All articles and features plus many regular columns appearing in the *Christian Science Monitor* are cited in this database. Although there are no abstracts in this file, the subject indexing is extensive. All regional editions are covered.

National Newspaper Index (Menlo Park, CA: Information Access Co.). 450,000 citations, 1979–

Intensive indexing is provided in this database for the following newspapers: *Wall Street Journal, New York Times, Christian Science Monitor, Washington Post,* and *Los Angeles Times.* All editorial matter, including obituaries, cartoons, letters to the editor, and features, is indexed. This is an archival file, derived from the NEWSEARCH database, which contains only the most recent month of indexing.

National Criminal Justice Reference Service (NCJRS) (Rockville, MD: Department of Justice, National Institute of Justice), 70,000 citations, 1972–

Ranging in its scope from reports on techniques for forensic investigation to articles on police force administration, this file covers all aspects of research and practice in law enforcement. In addition to books and journal articles, the database covers worldwide research reports, professional papers, and audiovisual materials.

National Rehabilitation Information Center (NRIC) (Washington, D.C.: National Rehabilitation Information Center, Catholic University of America). 3,500 citations, 1956–

The NRIC database contains citations to literature and materials in print and nonprint media covering research and professional practice related to the rehabilitation of persons with any type of handicapping condition. One will find here information on rehabilitation research dealing with both physically and mentally handicapped individuals. The file also includes information of use to the administrator of rehabilitation programs.

National Information Sources on the Handicapped (Washington, D.C.: U.S. Department of Education, Clearinghouse on the Handicapped). 300 records, current

A nonbibliographic file, NISH is an online directory of organizations and other resources providing information on handicapping conditions. Records in the file include organization name, address, and telephone number; a description of the aims and purposes of the organization; the handicapping conditions they serve; and the types of information disseminated by the group.

National Technical Information Service (NTIS) (Springfield, VA: National Technical Information Service). 1,000,000 citations, 1964– (some reports to mid 1950s)

Although the technical reports cited in this file deal principally with federally sponsored research in science and engineering, the NTIS database is also strong in areas of political, social, and economic analysis. The file overlaps to a small degree with the ERIC database in areas of educational research and with other mission-oriented government databases such as the DOE Energy Data Base and the GPO Monthly Catalog database. In social science fields the database will be a good resource for studies of economic development, demographics, political science, personnel psychology, and sociology. Although not the only vocabulary tool used in the file, the *Thesaurus of Engineering and Scientific Terms* will be a useful profiling tool for searching this file.

New York Times Information Bank (Parsippany, NJ: New York Times Information Service). 2,000,000 citations (NYT, 1969–; other sources, 1972–).

Originally developed as a research aid for reporters and staff writers of the *New York Times,* the NYT Information Bank provides exceptionally strong coverage of current events and topics of current interest in the world. The database contains abstracts and detailed indexing for all news stories and other editorial matter appearing in the Late City edition of the *New York Times* since 1969. Since 1972 the *NYT* abstracts have been supplemented by abstracts of items selected from a diverse group of about sixty other newspapers and periodicals such as the *Christian Science Monitor,* the *Financial Times of London, Harvard Business Review,* and *Scientific American.* Indexing terminology is drawn from the *Information Bank Thesaurus and User Guide,* created and maintained by the staff of the New York Times Information Service. Users will find this an invaluable resource in achieving good quality search results.

New York Times Online (Parsippany, NJ: New York Times Information Service). 240,000 records, 1980–

This file, which is updated daily, contains the complete text of all news stories and editorials that have appeared in the Late City edition of the *New York Times.* The database now provides subject indexing and brief summaries as well.

Newspaper Index (Wooster, OH: Bell & Howell, Micro Photo Division). 1,400,000 citations, 1976–

Newspaper Index provides comprehensive coverage of twenty-one U. S. newspapers including eleven black newspapers. Local, regional, national, and international news is covered from sources such as the *San Francisco Chronicle,* the *Houston Post,* the *New Orleans Times-Picayune,* the *Baltimore Afro-American,* and the *Chicago Defender.* No abstracts are available in the database.

NEWSEARCH. (Menlo Park, CA: Information Access Corporation). Current month only, updated daily

The initial indexing file for five other databases, NEWSEARCH contains citations for articles, news stories, and other items appearing in over 1,400 newspapers and periodicals. Business, legal, and general interest topics are included along with book, theater, and music reviews. Each month citations are tranferred from NEWSEARCH into Magazine Index, National Newspaper Index, Legal Resource Index, Management Contents, and Trade and Industry Index.

NICEM (Los Angeles, CA: National Information Center for Educational Media). 331,122 citations, biennial replacements

The computer equivalent of the *National Information Center for Educational Media Index,* this database consists of descriptions of audiovisual materials for use in a wide range of educational settings. Materials appropriate for all levels from preschool through postgraduate training are included. Specific media covered are 16mm films, 35mm filmstrips, overhead transparencies, audiotapes, videotapes, phonorecords, film cartridges, and slides.

NICSEM/NIMIS (Los Angeles, CA: National Information Center for Educational Media). 39,100 citations

This database, corresponding to the National Instructional Materials Information System, contains references to audiovisual and brailled media and to equipment and educational systems for use with handicapped children. All subject areas ranging from language arts and social studies to fine arts and sciences are included.

PAIS International (New York: Public Affairs Information Service). 150,000 citations, 1972–

Corresponding to the *Public Affairs Information Service Bulletin* and the *PAIS Foreign Language Index,* this database covers all areas of current affairs, including government affairs, economics, sociology, law, and other related fields. Materials indexed range from journal articles and published congressional hearings to other monographs from state governments or commercial publishers. In addition to keywords, many citations also contain brief annotations that improve their retrievability online.

POPLINE (Baltimore, MD: Johns Hopkins University, Population Information Program and others). 90,000 citations, 1970–

Produced jointly by Johns Hopkins and Columbia Universities, POPLINE provides searching of citations and abstracts of the world's literature on family planning, fertility, and health issues related to the family. The scope of the file extends to legal and policy considerations as well. The file is indexed using the *POPLINE Thesaurus* (1981).

Population Bibliography (Chapel Hill, NC: University of North Carolina, Carolina Population Center). 60,000 citations, 1966–

The entire range of periodical and monographic literature is indexed for this file, which provides access to all aspects of population studies. Significant coverage of studies on abortion, demography, fertility, population policy, and related areas. Emphasis in the file is on the social and economic aspects of population studies rather than their biomedical aspects. Geographic coverage emphasizes the United States and developing countries.

PSYCHINFO (Washington, D.C.: American Psychological Association). 400,000 citations, 1967–

Journal literature from nearly 1,000 periodicals plus monographs, reports, and dissertations are covered by PSYCHINFO. All areas of psychological theory, research, and practice are included. Records contain both indexing terms drawn from the *Thesaurus of Psychological Index Terms,* numeric classification codes, and substantial abstracts. The file contains all references published in *Psychological Abstracts,* and since 1980 many additional monographs have been recorded in the database only.

PTS International Forecasts (Cleveland, OH: Predicasts, Inc.). 400,000 citations, 1971–

Economic, demographic, and business forecasts for all countries outside the United States constitute this database. Over 1,000 sources are scanned for entries in the file, including governmental reports, company statistical reports, and publications from international agencies.

PTS International Time Series (Cleveland, OH: Predicasts, Inc.). 141,000 citations, 1948–

Predicasts, Inc., the publisher of both *Worldcasts Composites* and *Worldcasts Basebook,* has combined the information in these two printed tools into this database. It provides access to historical data from some 125,000 time series for all countries of the world, plus time series data and projections to 1990 for 50 key series in 50 major contries. Annual data usually extend back to 1957, with selected series going back to 1948. Topics covered include gross national product, income, production, employment, energy, and other such economic statistics.

PTS U.S. Forecasts (Cleveland, OH: Predicasts, Inc.). 260,000 citations, 1971–

The database contains statistics on U. S. business, economics, and demographics as they appear in government publications, business reports, and commercial publications. Baseline data are provided for most items in the file along with short-term and long-term forecasts.

PTS U.S. Time Series (Cleveland, OH: Predicasts, Inc.). 45,000 citations, 1957–

Predicasts Basebook and *Predicasts Composites* are merged in this online file, which provides access to some 37,000 series on production, consumption, prices, and activity in various industries in the United States. Historical data and projections are also included for 500 key time series on topics such as demographics, GNP, employment, production in specific industries, and prices.

Quebec (Quebec, Canada: Microfor, Inc.). 170,000 citations, 1977–

The machine-readable version of *Index de l'actualité vue à travers la presse écrite,* this file contains citations to all news articles, columns, editorials and other information appearing in three Quebec newspapers: *Le Devoir, La Presse,* and *La Soleil.* All entries and indexing in the file are in French.

Resources in Computer Education (Portland, OR: Northwest Regional Educational Laboratory). 2,000 citations, 1979–

Prepared by the Northwest Regional Educational Laboratory in Oregon, the RICE database provides citations to information about and evaluations of computer hardware and software being offered or now being used in school classrooms. The file contains entries both for producers of goods and/or services related to computer education and for the materials now available. Entries for the software are quite lengthy, allowing the searcher to retrieve information by type of hardware used, the subjects covered, the grade level, instructional objectives, and the answers to a number of standardized evaluative statements. Indexing terminology is drawn from the *Thesaurus of ERIC Descriptors.*

Resources in Vocational Education (Columbus, OH: National Center for Research in Vocational Education). 4,500 citations, 1976–

A nonbibliographic database, RIVE provides for the searcher descriptions of recent research and/or demonstration projects in vocational education. Records in the file are indexed by subject using the *Thesaurus of ERIC Descriptors* and by more than a dozen other categories of information such as funding source, time period covered, amount of grant, etc.

School Practices Information File (Latham, NY: Bibliographic Retrieval Service, Education Service Group). 6,000 citations, current

The School Practices Information File is a record of project summaries, program descriptions, and materials now being developed or tested in schools. Database records provide a descriptive abstract, subject indexing from the *Thesaurus of ERIC Descriptors,* and administrative/organizational information. All areas of educational practice and all types and levels of students are included in the file.

Social SCISEARCH (Philadelphia, PA: Institute for Scientific Information). 1,100,000 citations, 1972–

An enormous, multidisciplinary file covering all aspects of the social sciences, Social SCISEARCH provides access to key journal literature in all social science disciplines. Some 1,000 core journals in fields such as sociology, education, economics, and political science are indexed cover-to-cover; other items are selected from over 2,000 additional journals in the pure and applied sciences. Many significant books are included as well. This database also provides a unique method of searching literature through its association (via bibliographic footnotes) with previously published work. All footnote citations in current articles have been keyed into the database records, thereby allowing the searcher to retrieve relevant new references simply because they cite an earlier paper on the topic being studied. Subject access is limited, however, to words used in authors' titles, a distinct problem in searching some topics in the social sciences.

Sociological Abstracts (San Diego, CA: Sociological Abstracts, Inc.). 120,000 citations, 1963–

International research in sociology and other related social sciences is covered in this file. Items are selected from some 1,200 journals and other publications each year. Abstracts of papers presented at professional sociological meetings are also included. Subject coverage extends to sociological theory and methods, demographic studies, social phenomena and problems, and to sociologically oriented research of special populations. Abstracts are of substantial length.

Sport (Ottowa, Canada: Sport Information Centre). 45,000 citations, 1979–

The computer equivalent of the Canadian Sport Information Centre's *Sport and Recreation Index,* this database provides coverage of both journal and monographic literature on all aspects of individual and team sports. Materials in the file include primarily English- and French-language publications. Subjects represented include coaching, training techniques, equipment, sports injuries and treatment, and sports education.

United States Political Science Documents (Pittsburgh, PA: University of Pittsburgh, NASA Industrial Applications Center). 16,000 citations, 1975–

Research papers appearing in some 120 American journals are scanned for this file. All areas of political science as well as the disciplines of law, economics, public administration, and diplomacy are included. Records contain substantial abstracts and numerous indexing terms drawn from the *Political Science Thesaurus.*

UPI News (New York: United Press International). 4,000 records, 1983–

A full text database containing the final versions of United Press International wire stories, UPI News is a frequently updated source of current political, social, economic, and business information. The entire text of the news releases, running to several hundred words, is searchable.

U.S. Public School Directory (Washington, D.C.: U.S. Dept. of Education, National Center for Educational Statistics). 80,240 records, current

This nonbibliographic file provides access to highly categorized directory information on public elementary and secondary schools in the United States and its territories. In addition to its obvious usefulness as an aid to specific information about a single district, the database offers many potentials for quantitative analysis of American public education, enabling the searcher to generate lists of schools meeting specific criteria such as size or location. It would, for example, be easy to produce a list of all schools in Iowa with less than 200 students, potentially a valuable resource for social science researchers using a survey research technique.

World Affairs Report (Stanford, CA: California Institute of Special Studies). 25,000 records, 1970–

The database consists of digests from Soviet publications such as *Pravda, Izvestia,* TASS, and *Literaturnaya Gazeta* plus other non-Soviet sources which state Soviet views of various world developments. Subject analysis on a country-by-country basis is provided in the records. An English language digest of each news story is provided along with the citation to the original language publication.

5
Physical Sciences and Engineering

Characteristics and Terminology

Among the academic disciplines that might use the computer to conduct library research, perhaps most blessed are the fields of physics, chemistry, earth and atmospheric sciences, and the many subdisciplines of engineering. In many of these fields the useful life of a paper is relatively short—ten to fifteen years frequently. Consequently, the time span covered by most computer literature retrieval systems enables physical scientists and engineers to use this technology to review a large percentage of the body of literature most useful to them. Instances occur, of course, in which older literature gains renewed importance resulting from a resurgence of interest in technologies or methods that had lain on the shelf for years. In those cases, and in a select number of physical science disciplines such as some areas of geology, the need for literature far exceeds the computerized resources available, but generally the online systems have particularly strong offerings for researchers in these fields.

Databases in physical sciences and engineering, although numerous, are usually well focused, and most files are well indexed. For library researchers this means that they can frequently get the information they need with a search of only one or two files, using terminology that is usually quite precise. Research in the growing number of interdisciplinary fields, such as bioengineering, may take the researcher into less certain waters, but even in those instances a computer search should normally provide rather thorough coverage of relevant papers, usually within the scope of a few databases.

The bibliographic tools available range from large general purpose resources such as *Engineering Index, Science Citation Index,* and *Government Reports Announcements and Index* to more highly focused works such as *Meteorological and Geoastrophysical Abstracts* or *Metals Abstracts.* In machine-readable form most of these sources can be searched back to the late 1960s or early 1970s. Almost without exception, the databases in this field supplement the author's title with a substantial keyword list, and most citations contain either a brief annotation or a longer abstract. The library researcher can, therefore, usually rely on the database to have a relatively large number of "hooks" that can be used to snare the needed papers.

The physicist, the geologist, and the engineer have an additional advantage over the social scientist or literary scholar in that typically the writing style in the fields of science and technology is straightforward and unadorned, even if sometimes rather pedestrian. Clarity of thought and felicity of expression are desirable in any communication, but the language of science is rarely allusive. As a result, the search strategist can usually achieve higher precision from queries of machine-readable files of science and technology literature than from files in the social sciences and the humanities. This is not to say, however, that there are no terminological problems for scientists and engineers who conduct library research.

The naming of substances and techniques, even in fields where there is general agreement, can be a challenge to the researcher's imagination. To specify for the computer all acceptable variants of nomenclature may require the inclusion of formulas, abbreviations, trade names, "official" names, and/or registry or other industrial standard numbers. To illustrate, a search through several science-technology databases for information on the physical and electrical properties of gallium-arsenic compounds required over forty terms, including molecular formulas, Chemical Abstracts Service registry numbers, and a number of general search terms entered both in their fully spelled-out forms and as abbreviations. Figure 5-1 shows a portion of the strategy required for such a search.

Searches for literature on substances with complicated structures or large classes of compounds (e.g., polyolefins) require even more elaborate and lengthy strategies to insure complete coverage. In this particular regard online computer searching

GALLIUM ARSENIDE(S)	ELECTRIC(AL,ALLY)
GALLIUM MONOARSENIDE(S)	ELECT
RN=1303-00-0	PROPERT(Y,IES)
GA SUB 1 AS	PROP
ASGA	MELTING POINT(S)
GAAS	MP

Figure 5-1. Partial strategy for retrieving information on properties of gallium and arsenic compounds.

systems can be very misleading to the novice because they can produce results from almost any instructions they are given. Knowing when to question whether the results the machine is reporting are, in fact, a fair representation of all the relevant literature in the file becomes a matter of experience.

A second type of problem faced frequently by engineers is that of the "black box" search. The engineer has already determined that no device or system exists that can solve the problem under study and is looking for information about similar equipment, systems, or methods that might be used to develop a solution. For example, an agricultural engineer may need to develop a method for automatically counting eggs on a conveyor belt as they come out of a commercial hen house. No such device presently exists; so a search for literature about other industrial systems used for sensing and counting randomly placed items moving along a conveyor is needed. The engineer knows quite well what kind of information to look for, but enumerating all the possible word combinations that would enable a computer to retrieve a workable number of references is a task requiring both skill and a degree of artistry.

The search through the "black box" is in many ways, of course, characteristic of all modern research. Except for textbook writers, seldom does one write about an entire field such as bioengineering or even a narrower specialty such as prosthesis design. The professional literature is typified, rather, by reports of investigations on narrowly defined topics such as the development and testing of an artificial elbow joint controllable by servomechanism. The logic is unassailable for the author to report only what he did, and indexers, following the principle of specific entry, may assign very specific keywords when they prepare the citation. The result is a retrieval tool capable of retrieving materials at a high level of precision. The user of such a tool, however, may have to look under many headings in order to retrieve all the desired information. For example, the engineer trying to create a bibliography on the design of arm and hand prosthesis controls in general may have to search under every conceivable part of the arm from shoulder to fingers.

More frustrating perhaps than searches requiring the enumeration of many substances or parts are those where methodology is a variable of primary importance. The scientist may be well aware of the body of literature concerning a particular phenomenon or system carried out under traditional or "normal" conditions, but wants to find reports of that phenomenon or system observed under "abnormal" or nontraditional conditions, such as pressure between 50 to 100 psi, temperatures below 100 degrees centigrade, or at speeds in excess of 8000 rpm. On the other hand, it may be the apparatus or the testing technique that is the aspect of interest to the scientist, as in the case of a search for comparative data obtained from high pressure liquid chromatography when the technique most commonly used may be gas chromatography.

Searches with these types of requirements will prove difficult for two reasons. First, test conditions are usually described in the body of a paper and may not be referred to either by the author in the title of the paper or by abstracters or indexers in their additions to the citation for the database. Typically, titles, indexing terms, and abstracts focus on ends rather than means; so search strategies that rely on very specific methodological terminology may fail to retrieve many valuable papers. Much broader strategies, however, are just as likely to be unsatisfactory because they would retrieve too many irrelevant papers. The second source of frustration in searches of this type comes from the almost infinite number of ways in which conditions such as temperature or pressure could appear in a bibliographic citation. Since the computer is capable of searching only specific strings of characters, it can easily find papers exactly matching specified elements such as "100," "101," "102," etc., but it cannot make the determination that citations with elements such as "121.3," "150 to 225," or "at temperatures in excess of 99 degrees" also qualify for a search of papers citing results obtained at 100 degrees or greater.

Similar problems exist for earth scientists in trying to search time periods, height, depth, and geographical locations. Time, height, and depth reflect the same type of variability as pressure and temperature do in laboratory studies. Location poses additional problems in that geographical categories are frequently neither mutually exclusive nor universally defined. One could, for example, find useful citations on the same region of the central part of the country by searching "Kansas," "Ogallala Aquifer," "Ash Hollow Formation," more general terms such as "Plains States" or "Central United States," and in some instances even latitude and longitude coordinates.

Geographical designations in bibliographic citations are governed by a multiplicity of indexing policies. In many databases geography is specified in the keyword list only when the indexer judges that the author's purpose was to emphasize the location. Even when geography is stressed in a paper, consistent keywords may not always be added to the citation. Some databases have the policy of not adding standardized geographic keywords if terminology in the author's title states or implies the location. Take, for example, the title "Evaluation of Stormwater Drainage System for the City of Atlanta." An indexer following this policy, would in all probability not add "Georgia" as a keyword in the belief that it is common knowledge that Atlanta is in that state. Although such an assumption is probably true, the policy fails to account for the fact that the computer doesn't know this; so the searcher must resort to rather lengthy lists of terms if the highest number of papers dealing with a specific region is to be retrieved.

As illustrated by the example of terminology appropriate for the Kansas region, even when geographic designators are a part of indexing terminology, the choice of keywords may not always match the searcher's needs. Frequently the geographic descriptors applied are for political subdivisions such as counties, states, or countries. This approach is often quite satisfactory for the civil engineer designing a road project in Oklahoma or the remote-sensing specialist using photographs from the LANDSAT satellite projects. Environmental engineers or geologists, however, may find political subdivisions either too large or too small to define the areas they need to study.

Geographical descriptors are but an obvious manifestation of a more general library research problem of communication among writers and readers. Writers have the great advantage over readers of always working in a known context. As a result, the words they choose and the things they convey only by implication are woven into the fabric of the piece, and their meaning is understood in the context of the entire product, the paper as a whole. In contrast, readers, when they come to the library, must try to find the papers they need using only fragmentary clues—small swatches of the cloth, if you will. Sometimes the clues, the words and phrases relevant to their topics, provide a bold enough pattern to enable the readers to identify easily the relevant papers, but just as often they will find that the clues don't sufficiently define the topic and they either miss many relevant citations or have to edit the useful papers out of a much larger printout.

The simplest solution to these problems is, of course, to create a retrieval tool specific to the research field, one that uses the terminology used in that field and addresses the methodology and content of concern to specialists in that discipline. A great number of bibliographic tools have been created, of course, to address precisely these needs. Unfortunately no single resource can supply all the information an individual scientist or engineer will need, and tools aimed at more general research audiences or at specialists in other fields must be consulted.

For the computer search strategist the availability of numerous databases appropriate to a given research topic means that flexible profiles must be devised that can function efficiently in both specialized and more general contexts. The profile in Figure 5-2 illustrates the conceptualization and term selections

CONCEPT 1	CONCEPT 2	CONCEPT 3
Square Root(s)	Algorithm(s,ic,ically)	Computer(s,ized,ised)
Squareroot(s)	Extract(ed,ion,ing)	Hardware
	Binary	Software
	Array(s)	Microprocessor(s)
	Digital(ly)	Microcomputer(s)
	Modular(ly)	
	High Speed	

LOGIC:
Computer File: Concept 1 AND Concept 2
Mathematics File: Concept 1 AND Concept 3

Figure 5-2. Alternative strategies for a search on computer techniques for extraction of square roots.

planned for a search on computer methods for square-root extraction. The searcher has chosen to query both the INSPEC and the MATHFILE databases. INSPEC consists of the machine-readable version of *Electrical and Electronics Abstracts, Computers and Control Abstracts,* and *Physics Abstracts,* while MATHFILE is the computerized equivalent of *Mathematical Reviews.* Because the types of sources covered by INSPEC are slanted more often to the computer applications, which the researcher wants, the strategy proposes to combine only the first two groups of terms in searching that database. The resources of the MATHFILE database, in contrast, are expected to contain a higher percentage of more theoretical papers, which the researcher does not wish to see at this time; so the strategy proposes to add a third group of terms specifying computer applications.

Contingency planning like that outlined for seeking square-root extraction literature is a frequently used technique in computerized bibliographic searching. It provides greater efficiency in the conduct of online search sessions, and it frequently results in less expensive literature reviews. The tools described in the next section should prove valuable in writing effective profiles in scientific and technical databases.

Profiling Assistance

Terminology Standards

The need to communicate as precisely as possible has led scientists and engineers, through their professional societies, to establish standards for terminology within their disciplines. In some instances these standards have merely codified and defined the technical and scientific terms in common usage. In other cases, notably in chemistry and metallurgy, systems have been devised to create a common naming system so that substances with many names might be cited in a uniform manner.

The vast number of separate standards for metals and alloys has, for example, resulted in a bewildering array of designations for these materials. In order to impose some order on this often-confusing field, the Society of Automotive Engineers and the American Society for Testing and Materials published in 1975 the first edition of a handbook containing designations for over 1000 metals and alloys based on a Unified Numbering System (UNS). UNS provides a unique alphanumeric designator for each material registered and correlates that designator with the pertinent professional, governmental, and trade association names and standards for that substance. Although not yet universally used in the field, UNS numbers are appearing with increased frequency in professional literature, and as use of the unified numerical designators grows, the task of searching literature for particular substances will be made easier. The printed tool of greatest assistance in locating UNS designators is *Unified Numbering System for Metals and Alloys,* 2nd edition (Warrendale, PA: Society of Automotive Engineers, 1977).

Far more complicated than the naming of metallic formulations or alloys is the task of standardizing names for chemical compounds in general. The debates over chemical nomenclature have occupied the time of chemists for decades. Complicating the issues in this field is the strongly felt need for names that are both unique and heuristic. Uniqueness alone in a chemical name is obviously easy to achieve, but the task is infinitely complicated by the need for a system that also reflects a substance's structure and perhaps its relation to larger classes of compounds. Although universal agreement may never be achieved, a number of developments in the field will assist in searching chemical literature. The International Union of Pure and Applied Chemistry has established nomenclature standards that are widely used in the field. Two of their publications will prove useful in constructing name variants for compounds. They are *How to Name an Organic Substance* (New York: Pergamon Press, 1977), and *Nomenclature of Organic Chemistry* (New York: Pergamon Press, 1979). R. S. Cahn and O. C. Dermer's *Introduction to Chemical Nomenclature,* 5th edition (London: Butterworth's, 1979), is also a useful general guide to the naming of chemical compounds. The naming conventions followed by the American Chemical Society must, of course, never be ignored. Here the *Chemical Abstracts Index Guide* will prove indispensable. In constructing search profiles for *Chemical Abstracts,* users must remember that the editorial staff of Chemical Abstracts Service (CAS) reviews its indexing policies and practices at the beginning of the time period to be covered by a five-year collective index of *Chemical Abstracts.* Users of that tool, therefore, need to be aware that significant changes in the naming of substances may have occurred over the years, so they will need to consult the *Index Guide* for each five-year period they wish to search.

Even more important for searching *Chemical Abstracts* via computer is the CAS program for registering chemicals. In 1965 CAS established its Registry of Chemical Compounds, which is a record of each substance reported in chemical literature. Each substance entered into the register is assigned a unique registry number. Registry numbers are not designed to reflect either hierarchical or structural aspects: They serve purely as shorthand designators for a substance. They are used so extensively by indexers for *Chemical Abstracts* that a profile for that database will almost certainly need to include registry numbers. Figure 5-3 shows an entry from Chemical Abstracts Service's database, CA SEARCH, illustrating how registry numbers are used in indexing. The citation also clearly demonstrates the need for registry numbers in searches of chemical literature files. A chemical engineer needing to know about lanthanum oxide catalysts for the oxidation of carbon monoxide would, for example, have missed this citation if the registry number for that compound

```
8712359     CA:  87(16)12359v     JOURNAL
  Effect of the porous structure of rare earth element oxides on their
effectiveness in the oxidation of carbon monoxide
  AUTHOR:  Sultanov, M. Yu; Sadykova, Kh. A.; Klimova, G. N.
  LOCATION:  Azerb. Inst. Nefti Khim. im. Azizbekova, Baku, USSR
JOURNAL:  Azerb.  Khim.  Zh.     DATE:  1977   NUMBER:  2  PAGES:  16-21
CODEN:  AZKZAU   LANGUAGE:  Russian
  SECTION:
CA067002 CATALYSIS AND REACTION KINETICS
  IDENTIFIERS:  carbon monoxide oxidn catalysis, rare earth oxide catalysis
oxidn
  DESCRIPTORS:
Rare earth oxides...
     catalysis by, of oxidn, of carbon monoxide, porosity in relation to
Diffusion...
     in carbon monoxide oxidn., with granular rare earth oxide catalysis
Kinetics of oxidation...
     of carbon monoxide, with catalysis by rare earth oxides
Oxidation catalysts...
     rare earth oxides, for carbon monoxide, porosity in relation to
     activity of
  CAS REGISTRY NUMBERS:
1312-81-8 1313-97-9  12036-32-7 catalysis by, of carbon monoxide oxidn.,
     porosity in relation to
1308-87-8 1308-96-9 12036-41-8 12055-62-8 12060-58-1 12064-62-9
     catalysis by, of carbon monoxide oxidn., porosity in relation to
1308-96-9  1314-37-0 12032-20-1 12036-44-1 catalysis by, of oxidn. of
     carbon monoxide, porosity in relation to
630-08-0  reactions, oxidn. of, rare earth oxide catalysis of
1306-38-3 uses and miscellaneous,  catalysis by, of carbon monoxide oxidn.,
     porosity in relation to
```

Figure 5-3. Citation from Chemical Abstracts, volume 87.

(1312-81-8) had not been used. Indeed, without the registry number this article could have been retrieved only with a very broad strategy that included the phrase "rare earth oxides."

Because of their utility in succinctly identifying substances, registry numbers are becoming widely used in patent, life sciences, and engineering databases as well as purely chemical literature files. The *Chemical Abstracts Index Guide* will prove indispensable for looking up registry numbers, but other publications, such as the *Merck Index* and the *Toxic Substances Control Act Chemical Substance Inventory* (which lists commercially available chemicals), also list numbers for many hundreds of the more common substances. Although it lists no registry numbers, Cooke's *Chemical Synonyms and Trade Names,* 8th ed. (Oxford: Technical Press, 1978) can also provide assistance in profiling for specific materials.

A number of online chemical dictionaries are also available to assist in locating registry numbers, synonyms, and formulas. Their usefulness in looking up names associated with an individual compound is obvious, but files such as CHEMLINE, CHEMDEX, and CHEMSIS provide even greater assistance when the need is for names and numbers for groups of compounds. The earlier example of gallium-arsenic compounds is a good illustration of what these files can do. A user seeking all compounds with at least one gallium and one arsenic atom need only key in those elements and the online system can retrieve all citations whose formulas contain both. The online systems providing access to CHEMSIS and CHEMDEX, in fact, have developed methods by which entire groups of registry numbers can be transcribed into a search profile automatically, a feature than can prove extremely cost effective.

Although the naming of substances may prove to be among the most troublesome profiling tasks, professional groups dealing with other subjects have also grappled with terminology. Two examples will serve to illustrate the type of publications search profilers will find useful. The *IEEE Standard Dictionary of Electrical and Electronic Terms,* 2nd ed. (IEEE Standard 100-1977) (New York: Institute of Electrical and Electronic Engineers, 1977) lists and defines terminology in the field of electrical engineering. It will be useful for checking on abbreviations, variant word forms, and synonyms. A similar service for civil and mechanical engineers is performed by the *Glossary of ASTM Definitions,* 2nd. ed. (PCX103-508073-42) (Philadelphia: American Society for Testing and Materials, 1973).

Thesauri

The most successful indexing systems employ subject authority control, that is, a well cross-referenced list of authorized terms to describe the works entered into that database. In printed form thesaurus entries typically display indexing terms along with their associated terms. Figure 5-4 is an entry from the U.S. Department of Energy's *Energy Data Base Subject Thesaurus,* which is similar in its organization to most thesauri. The entry term is defined or the limits of its applicability for indexing are stated in the scope note (in parentheses). Terms following the USED FOR

SHELL MODELS [01]
(Nuclear shell models only; for electron shell models use ELECTRONIC STRUCTURE.)

UF	*Models (Shell)*
BT1	Nuclear Models
BT2	Mathematical Models
NT1	Governor Model
NT1	Interacting Boson Model
RT	Aligned Coupling Scheme
RT	Broken-Pair Approximation
RT	Elliot Model
RT	Talmi Integrals
RT	Weak-Coupling Model
RT	Wilkinson Theory

Figure 5-4. Entry from the Energy Data Base Subject Thesaurus.

(UF) designator are synonyms not authorized for use in indexing materials; materials appropriately described using those terms will be assigned the entry term. The terms listed after the Broader Term (BT), Narrower Term (NT), and Related Term (RT) designators are other acceptable indexing terms associated with the boldface entry in the manner indicated by their names. Broader and narrower relationships are obvious; related terms are associated with the entry term, but not in any hierarchical manner.

In using a thesaurus to select search terminology for an online query the user must remember that the use of a particular subject term will not, in most systems, retrieve items indexed using other terms listed under the chosen term. Thus a searcher who entered "Shell Models" could not expect also to retrieve a reference indexed using "Talmi Integrals," which is a related term (RT) under the former term. Both terms would need to be keyed in if both ideas are desired. Notable exceptions to this general rule are the National Library of Medicine's MEDLINE files and the Department of Energy's Energy Data Base, both of which provide a form of automatic hierarchical searching (see database descriptions).

Although the list is by no means exhaustive, the six thesauri described here are representative of the larger number of such tools available. Useful in their own right as vocabulary authorities for some of the largest scientific-technical databases, these works also provide more general assistance for researchers who need aids for building search profiles in databases that lack good vocabulary controls.

- *Thesaurus of Engineering and Scientific Terms* (New York: Engineers Joint Council, 1967). This thesaurus was developed during the mid-sixties through the combined efforts of the Engineers Joint Council and the U. S. Department of Defense as a vocabulary control for the burgeoning literature of science resulting in part from the rapid growth in federal spending for research. It has been one of the primary terminological authorities used by the National Technical Information Service (NTIS), the clearing house for technical reports and selected technical publications resulting from U.S. government research and development expenditures. In addition to the relational displays of subject terms that constitute the body of the text, the thesaurus also provides a permuted index to individual words and a classified listing that arranges terms from the main portion of the volume into large categories corresponding to the numerical field groupings of the Committee on Scientific and Technical Information (COSATI). By consulting the classified list first, readers can see all authorized headings for a specific field such as optics and then consult the hierarchical displays to see additional related terms. A fourth section provides a strictly hierarchical display of terms from broadest to narrowest, so that users knowing only a broad, general term could easily determine any more specific terms that might be used to index items they might wish to read.

- *INSPEC Thesaurus,* 1981 (London: Institution of Electrical Engineers, 1980). First published in 1973, this thesaurus contains some 9,000 terms used in indexing materials for the INSPEC database which corresponds to *Physics Abstracts, Electrical and Electronics Abstracts,* and *Computers and Control Abstracts.* Both an alphabetic relational display and a broader-to-narrower hierarchical display are provided. Because the INSPEC database is produced in Great Britain, spelling and term selection follow British standards; this thesaurus will, therefore, prove to be particularly valuable to American users planning to query the file.

- *Energy Data Base Subject Thesaurus* (Oak Ridge, TN: U.S. Department of Energy, Technical Information Center, 1981) (DOE/TIC-7000-R5). Over 25,000 terms covering all aspects of energy research can be found in this thesaurus, which is the subject authority for the Energy Data Base and several other specialized files created by the Technical Information Center of the Department of Energy. A permuted index to individual words appearing as part of authorized subject terms is available in a separate appendix (DOE/TIC-7000-R5(APP)). In addition to its utility for profiling searches on the Energy Data Base, the thesaurus will prove a valuable aid for profile construction in physics, electronics, and environmental sciences as well.

- *SHE: Subject Headings for Engineering* (New York: Engineering Index, Inc., 1980). This work is the subject authority for the interdisciplinary abstracting service *Engineering Index* (COMPENDEX in machine-readable form). It contains over 12,000 entries for main headings and their related subheadings in all fields of engineering and closely allied disciplines. Although it contains numerous cross references to related terminology and many instructions regarding the proper form for indexing terms, it is not a hierarchical thesaurus in the mold of the other works discussed in this section. It will be, however, of inestimable help to those profiling searches for the COMPENDEX database.

- *Thesaurus of Metallurgical Terms*, 5th ed. (Metals Park, OH: American Society for Metals, 1981). This 182-page volume is the principal vocabulary tool for the joint Metals Society/American Society for Metals information services *Metals Abstracts* and *Alloys Index*. Approximately 9,000 terms for all aspects of metallurgy are displayed, ranging from properties and structure of metallic substances to fabrication techniques and specific applications for metals.

- *GEOREF Thesaurus and Guide to Indexing,* 2nd ed. (Falls Church, VA: American Geological Institute, 1978). Indexing terms for the *Bibliography and Index of Geology* and its related earlier publications have been interrelated and regularized in this thesaurus, containing over 12,500 entries. Geographic place names, systematic terms (for rocks, fossils, etc.), and general subject terms (for geologic features, processes, properties, etc.) are displayed with related terminology. Fifteen appendices provide ready reference lists of terminology ranging from a list of geologic ages to soil types.

Databases

The databases described in this section deal primarily with information in the physical sciences and engineering. Other databases may also prove valuable for searches in interdisciplinary studies. For example, the ERIC database will contain many references on the physical sciences and engineering as content areas of curricula or on the training of scientists and engineers, while business files such as ABI/INFORM or PROMT will be valuable in searches relating to management or marketing of engineering services and products.

American Men and Women of Science (New York: R. R. Bowker Company). 130,000 records, 1979–

This nonbibliographic database provides the biographical information available in the printed reference work of the same name. In addition to providing access by names, the online file makes possible the selection of individuals meeting any of a number of specific criteria, for example, noteworthy physicists with PhD's from Stanford who are now living in Virginia or Maryland.

APILIT (New York: American Petroleum Institute, Central Abstracting and Indexing Service). 375,000 citations, 1964–

The American Petroleum Institute's literature file, APILIT, provides ready access to all aspects of worldwide petroleum-refining research and operations. Publications covered in the file include trade and professional journals, reports, and conference publications. For users not subscribing to API services, access to the file is presently limited to three hours connect time per year.

APIPAT (New York: American Petroleum Institute, Central Abstracting and Indexing Service). 95,000 citations, 1964–

Covering the patent literature in the technologies and processes of petroleum refining, this database supplements the American Petroleum Institute's literature database APILIT. Patents from the following countries are covered: United States, Belgium, Canada, France, Germany, Great Britain, Japan, the Netherlands, and South Africa.

APTIC (Research Triangle Park, NC: U.S. Environmental Protection Agency, Air Pollution Technical Information Center). 89,000 citations, 1966–1978

The database of the Environmental Protection Agency's Air Pollution Technical Information Center provides comprehensive coverage of air pollution research and management. Both socioeconomic and technical aspects of the subject are covered. The file contains both journal and nonjournal references.

BHRA Fluid Engineering (Cranfield, England: BHRA Fluid Engineering). 120,000 citations, 1974–

The contents of the ten abstracting services of the British Hydrodynamics Research Association (BHRA) plus several thousand other publications are covered in this database. Some 1,000 journals, plus books and conference publications, are indexed and abstracted; coverage is international. All aspects of fluid flow and fluid dynamics, fluid technology related to energy extraction, fluid technologies in general, and the properties of materials are included.

CA SEARCH (Columbus, OH: Chemical Abstracts Service). 5,300,000 citations, 1967–

The enormous resources of *Chemical Abstracts* are searchable in this database, which allows subject access by title, by indexing terminology, by CAS registry number, and by a code scheme corresponding to sections of the printed tool. Literature in all languages, as well as U.S. and selected foreign patents, are included. Abstracts are not a part of the file, but the indexing for each record is very detailed. Effective searching of specific compounds in CA SEARCH will normally require the use of registry numbers since they, rather than compound names, are the principal indexing keys to the detailed level analysis provided by Chemical Abstracts Service.

Carbon-13 Nuclear Magnetic Resonance Search System (CNMR) (Delft, The Netherlands: Netherlands Information Combine). 9,000 records

For researchers using carbon-13 NMR techniques, the CNMR database provides factual information, derived from published literature, on carbon-13 NMR spectra. Searches can be conducted for data on known substances by name, formula, or CAS registry number for data on unknowns exhibiting particular shift patterns or with a specific structure.

CAS Online (Columbus, OH: Chemical Abstracts Service). 6,000,000 records, 1965–

The chemical search and display system of Chemical Abstracts Service (CAS), this database allows searching of the entire CAS Chemical Registry System by chemical structures and substructures. Users construct two-dimensional representations of the substances of interest to them, either by a special graphics terminal equipped with a computer stylus or through a series of commands at a regular typewriter-type terminal, and the system will then report back structural diagrams plus names, molecular formulas, registry numbers and the ten most recent references appearing in *Chemical Abstracts* for substances matching the search parameters.

CASSI (Columbus, OH: Chemical Abstracts Service). 50,000 records, current

The automated equivalent of the *Chemical Abstracts Source Index*, CASSI provides basic identifying information for scientific and technical publications in chemistry and related sciences. Records provide full title, standard abbreviation, basic publication data, and frequently a listing of holdings information from major libraries. Information is derived from sources identified in the seventy-odd years of work in *Chemical Abstracts* plus publications identified by BioSciences Information Service (BIOSIS), *Beilstein* (prior to 1907), and *Chemisches Zentralblatt* (1830–1940).

Chemical Evaluation Search and Retrieval System (CESARS) (Lansing, MI: Michigan Dept. of Natural Resources, Office of Materials Control). 500 records

A nonbibliographic database, CESARS contains up to 115 data elements on chemicals significant in the environment, especially chemicals found in the Great Lakes Basin. Data contained in the file include chemical and physical properties, acute toxicity levels, subacute and chronic effects, analytical methods employed, species studies, environmental fate, etc.

Chemical Engineering Abstracts (Nottingham, England: The Royal Society of Chemistry). 60,000 citations, 1970–

Over 100 of the major worldwide journals in the area of chemical and process engineering are abstracted for this database by the Royal Society of Chemistry. Materials in the file are both theoretical and applications oriented, covering all aspects of chemical engineering plus related areas in other engineering specialities. The CEA file corresponds to the printed reference work of the same name.

Chemical Reactions Documentation Service (CRDS) (London: Derwent Publications, Ltd.). 120,000 citations, 1944–

Prepared by Derwent Publications, Ltd., and derived from the *Journal of Synthetic Methods,* the CRDS database provides information about developments in the research areas of synthetic organic chemistry.

CLAIMS/CITATION (Arlington, VA: IFI/Plenum Data Company). 3,250,000 citations, 1947–

This file provides access to patents that have cited previous patents. Over 5,000,000 patent numbers that have been cited in U.S. patents since 1947 are indexed in this file, thus allowing users to trace the relationships or potential relationships between patentable works.

CLAIMS / CLASS (Arlington, VA: IFI / Plenum Data Company). 100,700 records, current

This database is an online dictionary and guide to the classification scheme of the U.S. Patent Office. It provides an easy method of determining appropriate patent classifications for searching other patent databases.

CLAIMS / COMPOUND REGISTRY (Arlington, VA: IFI / Plenum Data Company). 14,000 citations, current

An adjunct file to other databases of IFI/Plenum Data Company, this database provides access to the chemical nomenclature of compounds cited in patent literature since 1950. IFI compound numbers (similar to CAS registry numbers), molecular formulas, synonyms, and "official" names are available in the file. It will also be useful as an adjunct to other chemical literature files where help is needed in identifying compound names.

CLAIMS / U.S. PATENT ABSTRACTS (Arlington, VA: IFI / Plenum Data Company). 1,450,000 citations, 1950–

Chemical, electrical, and general and mechanical patents listed in the *Official Gazette of the U.S. Patent Office* are cited in this database along with references to equivalent Belgian, French, British, Dutch, and West German patents when that information is available. Chemical patents go back to 1950, electrical and mechanical patents back to 1963, and design patents back to 1980.

CLAIMS / UNITERM (Arlington, VA: IFI / Plenum Data Company). 1,450,000 citations, 1950–

Detailed indexing created from a review of the entire text of a patent on chemical substances is made available in this database. Forty or more terms are added for each record, thus making readily accessible information on chemical structures and polymers.

Cold Regions (Washington, D.C.: Library of Congress, Science and Technology Division and others). 75,000 citations, 1962–

The science and technology pertinent to the study of Antarctica and its surrounding areas are indexed in this database. In addition to studies of the natural world of Antarctica, the file deals extensively with topics such as the behavior of materials and equipment in cold regions or navigation and construction in such an environment. Materials include all publication types.

COMPENDEX (New York: Engineering Information, Inc.). 1,200,000 citations, 1970–

Covering international literature in all the subdisciplines of engineering, this database contains abstracts of leading journals, publications from professional engineering societies, and conference publications. The file is the computerized equivalent of *Engineering Index;* it offers access by controlled vocabulary terms, free-text terminology, and by a numeric code scheme. Since 1982, references to individual papers appearing in conference publications have been placed in a companion database, EI Engineering Meetings, and COMPENDEX contains only references to the conference or symposium publication taken as a whole.

Comprehensive Dissertation Index (Ann Arbor, MI: University Microfilms International, Inc.). 820,000 citations, 1861–

Based on the work appearing in *Dissertation Abstracts International* and its precursors, Comprehensive Dissertation Index contains citations to the dissertations required for doctoral degrees. The time period covered extends from 1861, when the first academic doctorate was awarded in the United States, to the present. Almost all U.S. dissertations are included, and the number of foreign dissertations is growing steadily. Subject access is principally through the title of the work and a descriptor added for the field in which the work was done. One can search also by name, institution, degree, and year; none of the records contain abstracts, although a citation to *Dissertation Abstracts International* is provided for those dissertations appearing in that work.

Conference Papers Index (Bethesda, MD: Cambridge Scientific Abstracts). 975,000 citations, 1973–

This database provides access to the papers presented at scientific and technical meetings around the world. Subject access is restricted to title words. The file provides information about authors' addresses, and where possible provides information about the availability of printed conference publications. Indexing in the file is minimal, relying almost exclusively on the titles of papers as the subject access point.

DISC (Latham, NY: Bibliographic Retrieval Service). 4,000 citations, 1982–

The DISC database, without a print equivalent, provides cover-to-cover indexing of some two dozen journals in the microcomputer field. Subject matter included in the file ranges from minicomputer and microcomputer hardware and software to management issues involved in the implementation of microcomputers in offices. More general subjects such as database structure and the organization of information are also included.

DOE Energy (Oak Ridge, TN: U.S. Dept. of Energy, Technical Information Center). 1,010,000 citations, 1974–

The principal database of the U. S. Department of Energy's Technical Information Center, this file contains journal literature citations plus references to the whole range of energy-related publications. All aspects of the energy situation are covered, from nuclear energy and fossil fuels to alternate energy sources and energy management. The file corresponds to the printed *Energy Research Abstracts* and other more specialized publications of the DOE Technical Information Center, and until recently it concentrated on the work conducted by the staff of the U.S. Department of Energy and its many contractors in government, industry, and academia.

Energy Bibliography and Index (EBIB) (College Station, TX: Texas A&M University Library). 20,000 citations, 1919–

Equivalent to the printed *Energy Bibliography and Index*, EBIB provides access to nonjournal literature in all areas of energy development, technology, management, and use. Coverage is worldwide and includes all sources of energy, from fossil and nuclear fuels to biomass energy sources. Materials are selected from the extensive energy collections of the Texas A&M University Library and extend back in time, in some instances, to the late 1800s. Entries contain substantial abstracts plus indexing terms drawn from the U.S. Department of Energy's *Energy Data Base Subject Thesaurus.*

EIMET (EI Engineering Meetings) (New York, Engineering Information, Inc.). 75,000 citations, 1979–

This database includes detailed indexing of individual papers presented at professional meetings and subsequently published in a set of proceedings. All subdisciplines of engineering are included. Records in this file do not contain abstracts, but fuller descriptions of the entire set of proceedings as a published entity can be obtained in EIMET's companion file, COMPENDEX.

Electronics and Computers (ELCOM) (Bethesda, MD: Cambridge Scientific Abstracts). 360,000 citations, 1977–

Covering journals, monographs, dissertations, and patents, the Electronics and Communications database provides indexing and abstracting in areas of electronics, electrical circuits and equipment, computing electronics and related applications areas. The file corresponds to two printed tools: *Electronics and Communications Abstracts* and *Computer and Information Systems Abstracts.*

Electric Power Database (Palo Alto, CA: Electric Power Research Institute). 9,500 citations, 1972–

Corresponding to the Electric Power Research Institute's (EPRI) printed *Digest of Research in the Electric Utility Industry,* this database provides descriptions of research and development projects relevant to the electric power industry. The subject matter covered by the file includes all aspects of electric power generation and transmission, from hydroelectric power to nuclear power plants, from the economics of energy to environmental assessment of power generation. Project descriptions are for research efforts already completed and for those currently underway.

Electric Power Industry Abstracts (EPIA) (Washington, D.C.: Utility Data Institute for Edison Electric Institute). 20,000 citations, 1975–

Prepared by the Edison Electric Institute, the EPIA database includes citations to all forms of published material from journal articles and conference proceedings to studies by regulatory agencies and Congressional hearings. Subjects covered encompass all aspects of electric power plants, their operation, and their impact on society and the environment.

ENERGYLINE (New York: Environment Information Center, Inc.). 45,000 citations, 1971–

Energy Information Abstracts in computerized form, ENERGYLINE provides online access to journal, report, and book literature in all areas of energy research, use, and conservation. Materials are selected for their contribution to understanding of various energy-related problems. The scope of the file includes both technical and scientific literature as well as publications addressing social and policy issues. Records in the database contain keywords, substantial abstracts, and broad subject coding.

ENERGYNET (New York: Environment Information Center, Inc.). 3,000 records, current

Key energy contacts are covered in this directory file. Individuals, government and corporate contacts, and energy-related associations are listed, and for each the file provides current address and telephone number. Entries are also enriched with descriptions of energy activities and/or narrative statements of goals pertaining to the energy field.

ENVIROLINE (New York: Environment Information Center, Inc.). 100,000 citations, 1971–

This database is the machine-readable equivalent of *Environment Abstracts,* which covers all aspects of the world's environment. Both technical literature in fields such as chemistry and engineering and policy-oriented literature covering social, economic, and legal aspects of the topic are covered. Publications selected for inclusion in the database range from journal articles to monographs, from technical reports to governmental publications. Some patents and selected rulings published in the *Federal Register* are also included.

Environmental Bibliography (Santa Barbara, CA: Environmental Studies Institute). 225,000 citations, 1973–

Over 300 periodicals are indexed in this file, which covers all areas of human ecology; energy research; air, land, and water resources; nutrition; and health. No abstracts are provided in the database, but keywords are generously added to increase the retrievability of references from the file. The database corresponds to the printed *Environmental Periodicals Bibliography.*

Fine Chemicals Directory (Poynton, England: Fraser Williams [Scientific Systems] Ltd.). 250,000 entries, current

This nonbibliographic database is an automated catalog of commercially available chemicals. Some 50,000 chemicals are included in the file and are made accessible by compound names and synonyms, molecular formulas, Wiswesser Line Notations, and vendors' names and their catalog designations.

GEOARCHIVE (London: Geosystems). 450,000 citations, 1969–

Without an exact printed duplicate, this database contains information found in printed tools such as *GEOCOM Bulletin, Geotitles Weekly,* and *Bibliography of Vertebrate Paleontology.* Material in the file is selected from over 5,000 journals, books, conference publications, dissertations, and technical reports. Some 100,000 geological maps are included as well. All aspects of geological research are included, from paleontology to petrology, from seismology and tectonics to geochemistry and geostatistics.

Geomechanics Abstracts (London: Imperial College of Science and Technology). 9,000 citations, 1977–

Equivalent to the printed *Geomechanics Abstracts,* the GMA database provides subject access to articles, reports, and government publications on rock mechanics, soil mechanics, and engineering geology. Retrieval capabilities in the file are enhanced through the addition of abstracts and descriptors for general subjects and the names of specific projects.

GEOREF (Falls Church, VA: American Geological Institute). 800,000 citations, 1967–

Containing references published in the *Bibliography and Index of Geology* and related publications from the American Geological Institute, this database provides comprehensive coverage of international literature in all areas of geology and its related fields. Over 4,500 journals, books, reports, maps, and dissertations are indexed using the *GEOREF Thesaurus and Guide to Indexing.* Particular attention is given to the assignment of keywords and codes for geographic areas. Precise latitude and longitude designators, for example, are searchable in much of the file. Although coverage is strongest for the literature since 1967, the database creators have endeavored to go back and create machine-readable records for landmark works prior to the beginning of the file.

INPADOC (Vienna: International Patents Documentation Center). 110,000 records, most recent 6 weeks

Corresponding to *INPADOC Patent Gazette,* this database provides current coverage of recently issued patents in forty-five countries. Records provide both full patent citations and patent equivalents in one or more countries. Records are classified using the International Patent Classification System.

INSPEC (Hitchin, England: Institution of Electrical Engineers). 2,100,000 citations, 1969–

Some 2,500 journals plus books, reports, theses, proceedings, and patents are scanned each year for inclusion in this file, which corresponds to the three parts of *Science Abstracts: Physics Abstracts, Electrical and Electronics Abstracts,* and *Computers and Control Abstracts.* Coverage includes theoretical-, research-, and applications-level materials. Each record contains a substantial abstract and keywords drawn from the *INSPEC Thesaurus.* British spellings and usage will prevail in the file, and the handling of subscripted or superscripted terms will require that the database user be familiar with file documentation from the online vendor.

International Software Database (Fort Collins, CO: Imprint Editions, Ltd.). 10,000 records, current

Both the expert computer user and the computer hobbyist will find descriptions of minicomputers and microcomputer software available for sale. Corresponding to the *Microcomputer Software Directory* and *International Minicomputer Software Directory,* the file provides a brief annotation of two or three lines plus descriptors for broad applications areas (education, financial planning, games, etc.) and for systems on which the software can be implemented.

ISI/COMPUMATH (Philadelphia, PA: Institute for Scientific Information). 250,000 citations, 1976–

All the significant editorial matter in nearly 300 journals and 40 multi-authored books plus other articles drawn selectively from the larger SCISEARCH and Social SCISEARCH files make up the ISI/COMPUMATH database. It encompasses theoretical and applied mathematics, statistics, computer science, and operations research. Searchers have the option of searching source references by author, institution, or title. In addition, they can search for all items connected through footnote citations to earlier work or to core papers in any of several "research-front specialties" (papers of scholars and scientists who are working at the forefront of their areas of specialization).

ISI/Index to Scientific & Technical Proceedings & Books (ISI/ISTP&B) (Philadelphia, PA: Institute for Scientific Information). 500,000 citations, 1978–

Containing everything in the Institute for Scientific Information's *Index to Scientific & Technical Proceedings* plus other citations drawn from multi-authored scientific/technical books, annual reviews, and review journals, the ISI/ISTP&B database provides comprehensive coverage of a valuable resource in scientific and technical communication. All major scientific and engineering disciplines are included. Individual papers and authors can be searched as well as the general editors and collective title or titles and other data associated with the conference publication taken as a whole.

ISMEC (Bethesda, MD: Cambridge Scientific Abstracts). 150,000 citations, 1973–

The *ISMEC Bulletin* (Information Service in Mechanical Engineering) attempts comprehensive coverage of all areas relevant to mechanical engineering and engineering management. Some 250 journals plus book and report literature around the world are scanned for references covering topics such as industrial engineering, mechanics, energy and power engineering, handling technology, and management aspects of most engineering subdisciplines.

Mass Spectral Search System (MSSS) (Washington, D.C.: National Bureau of Standards and others). 38,000 citations, 1966–

Both factual information and bibliographic data pertinent to research utilizing mass spectrometry are made available in this file. Substances covered in the file are identified by Chemical Abstracts Service name and registry number, synonyms, molecular formula, and molecular weight. In addition, mass spectral profiles are retrievable online by searching for the data on compounds of a known molecular weight or that have a given mass-to-charge ratio. Searches for unknowns can also be conducted in which the system can retrieve information on substances with mass spectral profiles most closely resembling the searcher's data.

Mass Spectrometry Bulletin (MSB) (Nottingham, England: The Royal Society of Chemistry, Mass Spectrometry Data Centre). 120,000 citations, 1966–

Citations in the MSB database are drawn from over 400 sources including journals, books, reports, conference publications, and abstracts. They cover not only information directly related to mass spectrometric research but also to allied fields such as instrumentation, molecular processes, thermodynamics, and reaction kinetics. Material in the file is prepared by the Mass Spectrometry Data Centre of the Royal Society of Chemistry.

MATHFILE (Providence, RI: American Mathematical Society). 350,000 citations, 1973–

The computer version of the American Mathematical Society's *Mathematical Reviews,* MATHFILE provides intensive indexing of some 400 key international mathematical journals and selected coverage of approximately 1,200 others. The file consists of bibliographic citations for the period 1973–1979 and citation plus the full text of the review or abstract from 1980 on. All areas of mathematical research and applications are covered in the database.

METADEX (Metals Abstracts and Alloys Index) (Metals Park, OH: American Society for Metals and The Metals Society [London]). 500,000 citations, 1966–

METADEX is a joint project of the American Society for Metals and the Metals Society in the U. K. covering the world's metallurgical literature. Well over 1,000 key journals are indexed and abstracted along with books, reports, and conference publications. Printed equivalents of the file are *Review of Metal Literature* (1966–1967), *Metals Abstracts* (1968 to the present), and *Alloys Index* (1974 to the present). All aspects of metallurgy are covered, including metallic properties, processes, applications, and metal-forming technologies. Access is provided using standard nomenclatures and a variety of commercial and professional coding schemes for metallic composition.

Meteorological and Geoastrophysical Abstracts (MGA) (Boston, MA: American Meteorological Society). 100,000 citations, 1972–

Research findings in meteorology, astrophysics, physical oceanography, hydrology, and related environmental sciences are covered in the MGA database. The file provides indexing of journal, monographic, and report literature. Abstracts are available in the file for all years except 1974 and 1975.

Microcomputer Index (Santa Clara, CA: Microcomputer Information Services). 15,000 citations, 1980–

Some two dozen journals covering microcomputer development and use are indexed and abstracted for this database. Coverage includes general information on the field, specific applications, product descriptions, and reviews of both books and software packages.

Military and Federal Specifications and Standards (Englewood, CO: Information Handling Services). 70,000 citations, current

This database is the online equivalent of the microfilm indexes to the following publications by Information Handling Services: *Military Specifications and Services, Military Standard Drawings,* and *Hot Specs.* It provides title, subject, and Federal Supply Classification Code access to the thousands of specifications, standards, and drawings central to the procurement process of the U.S. government and can provide useful design data for more general engineering problems. In addition to citations to the text of standards and specifications, the file also can provide lists of products and/or vendors (Qualified Products Lists) previously qualified as meeting the criteria for the product or service described.

National Technical Information Service (NTIS) (Springfield, VA: National Technical Information Service). 1,000,000 citations, 1964–

Technical reports emanating from the research and development efforts of government agencies and their contractors are cited in this interdisciplinary database. It corresponds to the biweekly *Government Reports Announcements and Index.* All the reports in the file are publicly available and unrestricted in their distribution. Subject matter covers all fields but the greatest emphasis is in areas of pure and applied sciences and engineering. The typical record in the file consists of bibliographic data, contract information, a substantial abstract, and a lengthy list of descriptors. The descriptors are drawn from vocabulary lists such as the *Thesaurus of Engineering and Scientific Terms,* the *Thesaurus of ERIC Descriptors,* and other thesauri used by specific governmental information centers.

NMRLIT (Bethesda, MD: U.S. National Institutes of Health, in cooperation with Preston Publications, Inc.). 35,000 citations, 1964–

Covering the world's literature on nuclear magnetic resonance, the NMRLIT database provides access to journal literature in the field by specific subjects and by nucleus studied.

Nonferrous Metals Abstracts (Wantage, England: British Non-Ferrous Metals Technology Centre). 120,000 citations, 1961–

Corresponding to the printed *BNF Abstracts,* this database covers all areas of metallurgy and metallurgical technology related to nonferrous metals. Materials covered include journals, monographs, reports, and conference proceedings as well as selected standards and British patents.

Oil and Hazardous Materials–Technical Assistance Data System (OHM-TADS) (Washington, D.C.: U.S. Environmental Protection Agency, Emergency Response Division). 1,150 records

Providing up to 126 pieces of information on the identification, properties, and handling requirements of oils and hazardous materials, the OHM-TADS database will provide technical assistance to users responsible for the safe handling or disposal of these substances. The data in the file are derived from published sources and may contain CAS name and registry number, synonyms and molecular formula, toxicity measures, physical properties, and recommended handling and/or disposal procedures.

PAPERCHEM (Appleton, WI: The Institute of Paper Chemistry). 175,000 citations, 1968–

The *Abstract Bulletin of the Institute of Paper Chemistry* in machine-readable form, PAPERCHEM contains references to patents and to the scientific/technical literature of the paper industry. Subjects covered include all aspects of raw materials, papermaking processes, and paper products. Citations are also included on several collateral fields such as packaging, graphic arts, and the chemistry of materials used in papermaking.

PATSEARCH (McLean, VA: Pergamon International Information Corporation). 850,000 records, 1971–

Pergamon International's database covering all U. S. utility patents since 1971, PATSEARCH also contains reissue patents since 1975, defensive publications since 1976, design patents since 1977, plus all patent applications made under the Patent Cooperation Treaty and published by the World Intellectual Property Organization. All fields of technology are covered. Through special contracting arrangements, users can also obtain drawings and chemical structures of the patented materials or substances on videodiscs that interface with the online database.

PIRA Abstracts (Leatherhead, England: The Research Association for the Paper and Board, Printing and Packaging Industries). 65,000 citations, 1975–

The PIRA database contains indexing and abstracting of journal and monographic literature on the paper and packaging industries.

It covers both scientific and technical literature on products and processes involving paper, board, printing, and packaging. References also extend into areas of economics and consumer behavior related to packaging.

Pollution Abstracts (Bethesda, MD: Cambridge Scientific Abstracts). 90,000 citations, 1970–

The sources and control of pollution in the environment are covered in this file, which includes journal articles, government publication, and technical monographs. Subjects in the database include air and water pollution, environmental quality, solid waste management, and pesticides.

Power (Washington, D.C.: U.S. Dept. of Energy, Energy Library). 30,000 citations, 1950–

Effectively an online catalog of materials to be found in the Energy Library of the U. S. Department of Energy, the Power database provides access to a wide range of books, conference proceedings, and other library materials. Subject matter extends into all areas of energy research and management including its history and the complex interrelations between energy technology and the environment.

Rubber and Plastics Research Abstracts (RAPRA) (Shrewsbury, England: Rubber and Plastics Research Association of Great Britain). 200,000 citations, 1972–

The Rubber and Plastics Research Association's database, RAPRA, covers the world's literature on polymeric materials, their properties, production, and use. The file draws primarily from journal and monographic literature; both trade information and scientific/technical literature are included.

SAE Abstracts (Warrendale, PA: Society of Automotive Engineers). 11,000 citations, 1965–

The technical aspects of automobiles and other self-propelled vehicles are indexed in this file. Materials indexed are papers presented at various meetings of either the Society of Automotive Engineers or the International Federation of Automobile Engineering Societies (FISTA).

Safety (Bethesda, MD: Cambridge Scientific Abstracts). 120,000 citations, 1975–

Safety Science Abstracts Journal in computer form, this database covers periodical, monographic, report, and patent literature on safety aspects in many fields. Topics covered include safety research and methods in areas such as transportation, environmental quality, and working conditions. The scope of the file ranges from safety technology and psychological factors to legislation and safety education.

Searchable Physics Information Notes (SPIN) (New York: American Institute of Physics). 200,000 citations, 1975–

All journals published by the American Institute of Physics (AIP) and other important U.S. physics journals, as well as AIP's translations of Russian journals, are indexed in SPIN. File records include author-prepared abstracts in addition to indexing terms. Subjects covered in the database include all aspects of theoretical and applied physics, astrophysics, astronomy, and geophysics.

Single Crystal Reduction and Search System (XTAL) (Washington, D.C.: National Bureau of Standards, Office of Standard Reference Data). 60,000 records, current

Corresponding to the National Bureau of Standards' *Crystal Data Determinative Tables,* the XTAL database provides both bibliographic and numerical information on crystal structure and behavior of organic and inorganic compounds. The types of information retrievable from the file include reduced cell parameters, space group numbers, calculated densities, etc.

Standards & Specifications (Bethesda, MD: National Standards Association, Inc. and others). 100,000 records, 1950–

The standards and specifications promulgated by government agencies and industrial or professional societies are indexed in this database. The publications covered in the file treat testing procedures, official terminology, performance benchmarks, safety measures, products, and other technological requirements. For some statements of specifications, the file also provides lists of qualified suppliers. File records contain information about the issuing organization, Federal Supply Classification code, and designators for whether the statement has been adopted as an American National Standard or as a standard for a United States government agency.

Structure & Nomenclature Searching System (SANSS) (Bethesda, MD: U.S. National Institutes of Health and U.S. Environmental Protection Agency). 230,000 citations, 1970–

The pivotal element in the Chemical Information System of the U. S. Environmental Protection Agency and the National Institutes of Health, the SANSS database is an online dictionary of substances appearing in the Toxic Substances Control Act (TSCA) Inventory, plus substances identified in other files of the Chemical Information System and over seventy other databases of the EPA and other federal health agencies. The file allows standard searching options such as CAS registry number, name fragments, molecular formulas, and synonyms. In addition, SANSS allows the user to specify a two-dimensional graphic structure of a molecule, and it will report those substances with matching structures.

Superindex (Boca Raton, FL: Superindex, Inc.). 2,000,000 entries, 1967–

The Superindex database consists of entries from the back-of-the-book indexes in hundreds of professional and reference tools from twenty-one major scientific publishing houses. Works from organizations and firms such as the American Chemical Society, CRC Press, Van Nostrand Reinhold, and the World Health Organization are included. This highly interdisciplinary file enables the searcher to identify quickly sources of formulas, tables, and particular facts. Entries in the file cite book title and page number.

Surface Coatings Abstracts (Teddington, England: Paint Research Association). 70,000 citations, 1976–

International literature from journals, books, patents, and proceedings is abstracted in this database. Subject matter in the file is research on paints and surface coatings of all types, including dyes, resins, solvents, inks, and other additives. Also included is literature on testing, handling, and marketing of surface coating products.

Textile Technology Digest (Charlottesville, VA: Institute of Textile Technology). 80,000 citations, 1978–

Some 650 sources including journals, books, theses, patents, and other publications are indexed and abstracted in this file covering all segments of textile operations. Each stage of the processing of fibers and textiles is treated along with information on home economics, clothing design, marketing, and management in the textiles industry.

THERMO (Washington, D.C.: National Bureau of Standards, Office of Standard Reference Data). 15,000 records

This nonbibliographic file provides factual thermodynamic data on over 15,000 inorganic substances. Among the elements available in the database are enthalpy of formation, heat capacity, and entropy as well as data on the physical state and crystal structure of the substances covered. The file can be especially useful for data needed to predict chemical reaction equilibria.

Transportation Research Information Service (TRIS) (Washington, D.C.: Transportation Research Board). 175,000 citations, 1968–

Both published literature (from journals and books) and reports and descriptions of research effects in transportation constitute the TRIS database. All modes of transportation are covered, from air carriers and highway traffic to rail hauling and maritime transport. Subjects covered in the file range over the entire spectrum of transportation research, including highway design, traffic management techniques, safety, and transportation economics. The file is created from records prepared from research information systems for each of the major transportation modes plus records selected from the printed *Highway Safety Literature Abstracts.* Records in the file are heavily indexed and typically contain substantial abstracts.

TSCA Plant & Production (Washington, D.C.: U.S. Environmental Protection Agency, Office of Toxic Substances). 127,000 records, 1979

This closed file provides nonconfidential information about chemical plants and their production of substances on the Toxic Substances Control Act Inventory. Records contain the name and address of the chemical producer, the CAS registry number, amount of each listed chemical produced at the site, and other manufacturing and import data.

TULSA (Tulsa, OK: University of Tulsa, Information Services Division). 324,000 citations, 1965–

International literature from journals, monographs, and patents on oil and gas exploration and production constitute this database, which corresponds to the printed *Petroleum Abstracts.* The technology of exploration, drilling, and production plus research in related fields such as geophysics, pollution, and transportation are covered in the file. Records contain both indexing terms and substantial abstracts to aid retrieval.

USCLASS (McLean, VA: Derwent, Inc.). 4,700,000 records, 1970–

This file is an online searching aid for identifying proper classification numbers for U. S. patents. The information is drawn from the classifications developed for patents from the earliest ones issued in 1790 to the present and is regularly updated to reflect new and revised categories.

U.S. Patents Alerts (USPA) (McLean, VA: Derwent, Inc.). 850,000 citations, 1970–

The information normally found on the first page of a U.S. patent plus patent claims and other data are provided in this file. Documents covered represent U. S. patents, continuations, divisionals, and defensive documents since 1970.

WATERDROP (Distribution Register of Organic Pollutants in Water) (Athens, GA: U.S. Environmental Protection Agency, Environmental Research Laboratory). 20,000 records, 1970–

Both bibliographic and factual data are made available in this file, which covers distribution studies of organic pollutants that are present in water. Records provide information about conditions under which the sample was taken, the analytical methods employed, concentrations detected, and a number of other data elements reported.

Water Resources Abstracts (Washington, D.C.: U.S. Dept. of the Interior, Water Resources Scientific Information Center). 175,000 citations, 1968–

Corresponding to the U. S. Department of the Interior's *Selected Water Resources Abstracts,* this file contains journal and monographic literature plus reports, patents, and proceedings, covering all aspects of water, its management, and use. Records contain numerous keywords drawn from the *Thesaurus of Water Resources Terms* and rather lengthy abstracts, which improve retrievability of information. Materials represented in the file are published primarily in English and are particularly strong in the areas of water planning, water cycle, and water quality.

WATERNET (Washington, D.C.: American Water Works Association). 6,500 records, 1971–

Primarily a machine-readable index to the publications of the American Water Works Association, WATERNET covers technical- and professional-level publications on topics such as water management, quality controls, standard testing methods, etc. In addition to publications by AWWA itself, the file contains a selection of articles and reports from agencies, water utilities, and research centers around the world.

WELDASEARCH (Abington, England: The Welding Institute). 70,000 citations, 1967–

Publications ranging from articles and books to patents and theses are indexed in this file, which covers the core literature of welding research and technology. Subject matter for the file extends from discussions on welding technology for metals and plastics to studies in collateral fields such as metallurgical properties or thermal cutting. Coverage is worldwide.

World Aluminum Abstracts (Metals Park, OH: American Society for Metals). 100,000 citations, 1968–

A production of the American Society for Metals, the World Aluminum Abstracts database covers international technical literature on all aspects of aluminum production, processing, and fabrication. Not only studies on the extraction of alumina and properties of the metal, but also literature on casting technology and metal finishing is included.

World Textiles (Manchester, England: Shirley Institute). 120,000 citations, 1970–

World Textiles Abstracts in computer form, the database contains references to international journals, standards and patents from the United States and Great Britain, statistical publications, reports, and proceedings. All aspects of fibers and their manufacture into textile goods is the subject matter for the file. In addition, one can use the database to locate information on the textile industry and the use of fabrics in a number of different applications such as medicine and inflatable structures.

X-Ray Crystallography Search System (CRYST) (Cambridge, England: Crystallographic Data Centre). 28,000 records, 1935–

The CRYST database contains both bibliographic and factual information, derived from published literature, on the crystallography of some 38,000 organic or organometallic compounds. Users of the file can search not only by name, CAS registry number, and formula, but also by various parameters related to the unit crystal cell. In addition to bibliographic and textual information on the substances, the database can also provide graphic representations online.

Zinc, Lead, and Cadmium Abstracts (ZLC) (London: Zinc Development Association). 20,000 citations, 1970–

A composite database, ZLC corresponds to the Zinc Development Association's *Zinc Abstracts, Lead Abstracts,* and *Cadmium Abstracts.* It covers literature on the chemistry, production, and use of these three metals. Primarily consisting of references to scientific and technical reports appearing in journals, technical monographs, and patent literature, the ZLC database also provides some data tables, statistical summaries, and digests of industry news. Although the bulk of the file covers the time period from 1970 forward, the literature on galvanizing extends back to 1950.

6
Business Literature

Characteristics and Terminology

One can argue convincingly that the entrepreneur's or the professional manager's primary job is the integration of information and resources into useful and profitable products and services. The possible permutations of facts, ideas, and human or material resources are virtually limitless. The information needs of businesses and the resources for meeting those needs are likewise enormous. Internally generated resources such as management information systems (MIS) or financial accounting systems are usually highly integrated, collecting and organizing data that comes from operations of a single firm. Management and accounting systems, when they operate well, are characterized by internal consistency and predictability about the information that can be produced from the data in the systems. Information external to the operations of a firm is vital to good decision making as well, but finding it in a timely fashion and organizing it for use requires both diligence and imagination. The business environment is profoundly affected by a multitude of forces. Internally, business managers must deal with the physical and psychological dimensions of the workplace. Thus, information on ergonomics, industrial psychology, labor relations, and organizational behavior becomes valuable to them. They must also, however, deal with external forces such as the general economic climate, existing or proposed governmental regulations, and consumer attitudes. Nor can they ignore for very long information about new technology or the structure of and activity within their industry; they must know who their competition is and how they can best meet their challenges.

Unlike internally created information systems, the resources available to provide the answers to the problems just described are not well integrated. They are dispersed among a large variety of materials, ranging from publicly available government documents to highly priced proprietary marketing reports, from straightforward statistical compilations to rather cryptic statements buried in the middle of the *Wall Street Journal*. It is for these kinds of resources that the business manager turns to the librarian or information specialist who must be able from time to time to produce amazing feats of bibliographic legerdemain.

In order to serve its clientele adequately a business information center must be able to access both the reports of pure research in areas as wide ranging as color perception to thin film chromatography and the applied, mission-oriented publications describing innovations and operating results of major competitors. Because of the diversified needs of their users, business librarians have typically spent a good deal of their time contacting other libraries and information centers trying to gain access to materials not available in their own libraries, which quite frequently are rather small. While online computer search services have by no means reduced the need for borrowing materials among business libraries, they have dramatically increased the capabilities of business information specialists to identify materials relevant to their client's needs.

There are today a large and growing number of online databases relevant to the research needs of business users. Many of the business-oriented files go well beyond purely bibliographic data to provide specific pieces of information. These nonbibliographic databases include directory information, time series statistics, annual report data, up-to-the-minute business news, and governmental regulations. The bibliographic resources are equally broad in their coverage, with both general purpose and industry-specific databases available for searching.

In approaching a business database one needs to remember that he is looking at a body of literature that borrows heavily from many academic disciplines. As a result, the most appropriate database to search may not be a "business" file at all, but rather a scientific/technical file such as CA SEARCH or a social science database such as PSYCHINFO. The library researchers in business must, therefore, be particularly sensitive to terminology unique to the academic disciplines that provide the theoretical and empirical underpinnings for much of business literature. They must also be aware of words and phrases that have emerged in the practical literature aimed at businesspeople. This is particularly true in the more technical areas such as accounting, finance, and industrial engineering, but even the more general literature of management and marketing is generously peppered with specialized terms and buzzwords.

Even the most careful business researcher, however, will experience a good deal of frustration with terminology simply because so much of it consists of nondistinctive, common words used in special ways—words such as "return," "interest," "distribution" and so forth. While context gives more than adequate clues to the reader of an entire page of textual matter, the computer does not provide that luxury; so the searcher has to try to anticipate all the possible contextual clues, rarely with perfect success. As with writers in many other social sciences and humanities fields, authors of business papers are also frequently given to the use of "grabbers" in titling their works. Thus one may encounter titles such as "Feeding Time at the Zoo" or "The Elephant in the Boat: The U.S. and International Financial Agreements," which certainly do arrest the eye but can provide rather high levels of frustration to the reader scanning search results. Much of the problem of dealing with allusive or humorous titles is corrected by the addition of indexing vocabulary and/or abstracts to the bibliographic citation. Still, such language remains a stumbling block because it impedes one's assessment of the relevance of the article to the desired topic and it inevitably leads to the retrieval of many irrelevant citations.

Another frustration the library researcher in business is likely to encounter more frequently than researchers in many other disciplines is that of proprietary restrictions on information. Because the availability of good information can sometimes mean the difference between corporate success and failure, its flow is often closely controlled. At one extreme, some types of data that a researcher would like to have are simply not available because the firm in possession of those facts chooses not to report them to outsiders. An example of this type of information would be statistics of a firm's operating results on a product-by-product basis. Information about proprietorships, partnerships, and other closely held firms can be especially difficult to gather, since reporting requirements for such businesses are much less stringent than they are for larger publicly-held companies, which are regulated by the Securities and Exchange Commission.

In other instances, information services have been created for the express purpose of collecting and organizing business data into readily usable formats; they then market such information, usually at quite substantial fees of from several hundred to several thousand dollars per report. It is not uncommon for such reports to be cited in literature reviews, but their cost makes them difficult to obtain. Typical of such publications are the reports produced by marketing research firms such as Predicasts, Inc.

Even in more open literature, the business researcher may encounter policies that make it difficult to get information in the desired form. For example, information may be needed on individual company performance, and only data aggregated into large industrial segments, will be available, as is often the case when governmental agencies report on data gathered in surveys or censuses of business activity. In order to counterbalance some of these problems, the business researcher has to be especially ingenious in identifying the sources that will provide the desired information.

Profiling Assistance

Perhaps more than researchers in many scientific and technical fields, the business researcher needs to have available an up-to-date guide to databases. A particularly good one is *Directory of Online Databases* (updated quarterly) by Ruth Cuadra, David Abels, and Judy Wanger (Santa Monica, CA: Cuadra Associates, Inc.). Many of the most widely available online databases are covered later in this chapter, but *Directory of Online Databases* provides similar information on many more such files that will be of interest to a much narrower audience. It is especially strong in its coverage of nonbibliographic and numerical databases, that is, those files containing directory-type information, news items, statistics, and/or other factual information rather than merely citations to primary sources.

Having selected an appropriate database, the user can employ any of a number of techniques and vocabulary tools to construct a search strategy. Because business literature is so highly dispersed, predicting how relevant citations may have been indexed in a given secondary tool is often difficult. Using one or two papers known to be relevant to the topic can prove a valuable technique for retrieving other relevant citations. By calling up a known relevant citation and printing it online in a format that displays the indexing terms assigned to it, the searcher can quickly determine the terminology most likely to produce the best results in a search of the entire file. For the researcher without knowledge of any such relevant papers the bibliographies in a recent textbook covering that area may prove useful.

Known-item searching techniques can be helpful as well when citation referencing is deemed appropriate. Citation referencing has long been a standard research technique for attorneys and legal scholars as evidenced by the ubiquity of reference works such as the many editions of *Shepard's Citations*. With such a tool a researcher can, by using a known relevant citation, find other relevant cases that subsequently cited the earlier decision. This method of searching via association is used in a number of other bibliographic tools as well, notably *Social Sciences Citation Index* (*SSCI*). *SSCI* indexes hundreds of journals considered central to social science research, providing not only traditional author and subject searching options but also citation searching of all bibliographic footnotes appearing in indexed articles. Figure 6-1 illustrates a citation search for articles indexed during 1981 that have cited Peter Drucker's 1980 book *Managing in Turbulent Times*.

Thesauri and Database Guides

The level and quality of indexing in business databases varies widely; so the value of thesauri or guides to particular databases will also vary. In heavily indexed files such as ABI/INFORM, vocabulary tools will be essential for good quality retrieval. In other files relying more on the natural language of a summary

DRUCKER PF		Vol	Pg	Yr
80 MANAGING TURBULENT T				
DIMATTIA SS	LIBRARY J	106	530	81
FULLERTO.HN	MON LAB REV	103	11	80
HARRIS PR	TRAIN DEV J	35	18	81

Figure 6-1. Entry from cited reference section of Social Sciences Citation Index.

or the title used by the author, their utility is less certain. The thesauri and database guides described here are among the most useful.

- *Words That Mean Business*. Elizabeth B. Eddison and Lois B. Lyman, comp. (New York: Neal-Schulman Publishers, Inc., 1981). This list of some 3,000 terms for indexing and organizing business literature aims for a middle ground of specificity between the too-general headings common in most library catalogs and the over-specific terminology used in specialized indexing tools. Although it is not presently used as the vocabulary authority for any particular database, *Words That Mean Business* provides terminology at the generalist's level for all the major business specialties, such as strategic planning, management, marketing, accounting, communications, international business, computing, and industrial production. Subject term displays are supplemented by lists of principal agencies and organizations affecting business, major companies, currencies of the world, and standard subject headings.

- *ABI/INFORM User Guide* (Louisville, KY: Data Courier, Inc., 1980). This looseleaf reference work describes the bibliographic citations contained in the ABI/INFORM database. It provides guidance in constructing search strategies on the file, a list of journals indexed, and a lengthy thesaurus of terms and proper names used in indexing materials for the database. The focus is on terms and concepts needed by business executives and managers in all business activities, and although designed as a guide to a single database, it can prove useful for profiling in other business related files.

- *Predicasts Terminal System Reference Manual* (Cleveland, OH: Predicasts, Inc., 1982). Predicasts is a marketing research firm which, among its other services, indexes nearly 1,200 periodical publications of interest to business professionals. The *PTS Reference Manual* lists the terms, standard industrial codes (SIC's), and specialized "event" codes that Predicasts staff use to index materials for their numerous online files such as PTS F&S Indexes, PTS PROMT, and several statistical files. Two special sections describing search protocols for the PTS files as they are available on the search systems of DIALOG Information Service and Bibliographic Retrieval Service are also included in the manual. It is perhaps one of the very best sources for finding SIC codes since it provides both alphabetic and numeric access.

- *Management Contents Data Base Thesaurus* (Northbrook, IL: Management Contents, Inc., 1981). Really a user's guide for the database, this manual and its accompanying *Indexer's Manual and Dictionary* explain the policies followed in creating bibliographic records for the file, which abstracts some 500 publications. Terminology is displayed alphabetically in broadly categorized lists, without cross references or hierarchical groupings.

- *Political Science Thesaurus II*, revised ed., by Carl Beck, Thomas McKechnie, and Paul Evan Peters (Washington, D.C.: American Political Science Association, 1979). The database U.S. Political Science Documentation uses this thesaurus as its vocabulary guide. While the primary focus is on public policy and political science research, it will also prove a valuable source of terminology for business research in the areas of management, marketing, organizations, and economic policy.

- *Thesaurus of Psychological Index Terms*, 3rd ed. (Washington, D.C.: American Psychological Association, 1982). The PSYCHINFO database and the terms contained in this thesaurus will be of particular interest to industrial psychologists, personnel and training specialists, and managers seeking information about the psychology of business. Terms are appropriate both to business management (employee motivation, training psychology, etc.) and to consumer behavior (attitudes, perceptions, etc.).

Code Schemes

In addition to words and phrases as keys for identifying relevant information, numeric or alphanumeric codes can also contribute to improved searching in some databases. Most code schemes that are available in online databases allow the searcher to retrieve fairly large segments of literature with minimal keyboarding. In most instances the codes derive from the computer tags used to set up the major sections of the printed indexing service. By using a code such as 3690 in the PSYCHINFO database, for example, the searcher can easily pull into a strategy all the papers that have appeared in the "Marketing and Advertising" section of the printed *Psychological Abstracts*, regardless of what terminology the author or indexer may have used. By then intersecting that set of references with other sets on the specific aspect of marketing or advertising under investigation, the searcher can retrieve the desired information.

Not every database has such codes available, and even those that do use codes employ them in many different ways. Before using any code as part of a search strategy, searchers must always be sure that they understand how it is used, and particularly whether its use has been consistent throughout the period of time they will be searching. Several of the code schemes available in one or another business-related database are described here:

- Standard Industrial Classification (SIC) Codes. The Standard Industrial Classification system was created by the Federal Bureau of the Budget (now the Office of Management and Budget) as an aid to the collection and analysis of data. It is designed to cover the entire field of economic activity:

```
200 0000  FOOD & KINDRED PRODUCTS
201 0000  MEAT PRODUCTS
201 1000  Fresh Meat
201 1100    Beef & Veal
201 1110      Beef
201 1120      Veal
201 1300    Lamb & Mutton
201 1400    Pork, Fresh & Frozen
201 1500    Lard
201 1900    Slaughterhouse Products, NEC
201 1910      Hides & Skins
201 1911        Calf & Kip Skins
201 1912        Cattle Hides
201 1913        Sheep & Lamb Skins
201 1914        Goat & Kid Skins
201 1915        Buffalo Hides
201 1916        Horse Hides
201 1917        Pigskins
201 1918        Hides & Skins, NEC
201 1920      Fresh & Frozen Meats, NEC
201 1930      Glue Stock
```

Figure 6-2. Standard Industrial Classification code numbers.

agriculture, forestry and fisheries; mining; construction; manufacturing; transportation, communications, electric, gas, and sanitary services; wholesale and retail trade; finance, insurance, and real estate; services; and public administration. SIC numbers are hierarchically structured to permit their application at several levels of specificity. Figure 6-2 illustrates part of the hierarchy for food and food by-products. In many reference works, such as the Dun and Bradstreet services, these codes are applied at the specificity of four digits (e.g., Fresh Meat, SIC 2011). But others, such as the files produced by Predicasts, Inc., use longer, more specific codes that enable researchers to focus on much narrower lines of business.

The U.S. government publishes the SIC classification system in *Standard Industrial Classification Manual* (Washington, D.C.: Executive Office of the President, Office of

```
4000    ACCOUNTING, TAXATION, AND LAW

  4100  Accounting
  4110  Accounting firms and Accountants
  4120  Accounting policies and procedures
  4130  Auditing
```

Figure 6-3. Selection from ABI/INFORM classification scheme.

Management and Budget, 1972). The work is thorough, but updating has been extremely slow. Another excellent guide for finding these numbers is the *Predicasts Terminal System User Manual* (Cleveland, OH: Predicasts, Inc., 1982).

- COSATI Codes. The Committee on Scientific and Technical Information developed an alphanumeric scheme for arranging *Government Reports Announcements and Index*, the principal abstracting service of the National Technical Information Service. The codes divide the *GRA&I* into twenty-two major sections such as 05 (Behavioral and Social Sciences) or 12 (Mathematical Sciences). Each of the major sections is then subdivided into two or more subject specialties, such as 05C (Economics) or 05I (Personnel Selection, Training, and Evaluation). Although codes are generally too broad to allow precise retrieval, they can be very useful in establishing a general context for other search terms. By combining code 05I for personnel work, for instance, with keywords such as "computer assisted" or "computer aided," one could easily identify papers dealing with computer applications for personnel selection and training.

- ABI/INFORM Codes. In addition to its lengthy keyword list the ABI/INFORM database contains hierarchical subject and function codes. Each paper in the database is assigned code numbers denoting the business functions it discusses (accounting, finance, etc.), the type of treatment the paper provides (company specific, product specific, etc.), aspects of the business environment (economic conditions, social issues, etc.), or particular large industrial and market sectors. On the average more than two codes have been applied to each paper in the database. As Figure 6-3 illustrates, the classification scheme will enable searchers to use the codes to retrieve materials with either a broad or a narrow focus. By selecting all items with a code number beginning with 4, the user would get broadest retrieval and by selecting a more specific number, such as 4130, could restrict output to the narrower field of auditing. The combination of these codes with more specific word searches enables the searcher to focus search output much more efficiently.

Other databases such as PSYCHINFO or Sociological Abstracts also use coding schemes to help organize information; users wishing to search those files will be well advised to consult the documentation provided by the database producers. A brief discussion of the files can be found in Chapter 4.

Databases

As was indicated at the beginning of this chapter, business literature is eclectic, drawing information from many separate disciplines. In a sense, almost every database has some potential value for business research. Those described here are the databases available widely that contain the core of business literature. Other directories should be consulted for information about additional business literature files and those databases specializing in numeric information and computational services.

ABI/INFORM (Abstracted Business Information) (Louisville, KY: Data Courier, Inc.). 200,000 citations, 1971–

Focusing on literature that provides significant information to decision makers, the ABI/INFORM database draws selectively from nearly 600 business journals. All fields of business are covered. Items contain summaries of up to about 200 words plus additional subject category codes and keywords drawn from a controlled vocabulary list, the *ABI/INFORM Users Guide*. Information in this file will overlap significantly with that in the Management Contents database.

Accountants' Index (New York: American Institute of Certified Public Accountants). 100,000 citations, 1974–

The machine-readable equivalent of the American Institute of Certified Public Accountants' indexing tool of the same name, this database provides access to journal and monographic literature touching on all aspects of accounting and auditing research and practice. Included in the file are also references to the many discussion memoranda and accounting statements and interpretations of groups such as the Financial Accounting Standards Board (FASB).

ADTRACK (St. Paul, MN: Corporate Intelligence, Inc.). 325,000 citations, 1980–

Nearly 150 general interest magazines are reviewed for their advertising copy. Advertisements of at least one quarter page are indexed by product, company, subject, and other characteristics. Marketing and advertising professionals, especially, will find the information accessible here of value.

Advertising & Marketing Intelligence. (Parsippany, NJ: New York Times Information Service in conjunction with the J. Walter Thompson Company). 125,000 citations, 1975–

Indexing and abstracts for some five dozen journals are provided in this file, which covers the fields of marketing practice and research, consumer attitudes, advertising, sales promotion, and the media.

Banker (Wooster, OH: Bell & Howell). 30,000 citations, 1979–

This computerized index to the *American Banker* provides comprehensive coverage of the banking industry. Topics included in the file range from information on bank stock to discussions of security for data processing systems used in banking. The file corresponds to the printed *Index to the American Banker* published by Bell & Howell, Inc.

Business International / Data Forecasts (New York: Business International Corporation). 50 forecasts, current

This is a nonbibliographic database containing extensive narrative and statistical information on forecasts of social, political, economic, and industrial conditions in thirty-five countries. Coverage includes data on national income, production, imports and exports, capital formation, and banking conditions. Reports out of this file are typically very long.

Business International/Data Time Series (New York: Business International Corporation). 25,000 records, varying dates

Time series data on some 300 time series for up to 131 countries are covered in this nonbibliographic database. Official governmental and international organizations' publications are covered, plus many reports from Business International's own correspondents. Data included covers economic and industrial data, labor statistics, national accounts, and demographics.

Canadian Business Periodicals Index (Toronto, Canada: Micromedia, Ltd.). 30,000 citations, 1975–

Corresponding to the printed index of the same name, this file provides access to some 150 Canadian business publications, such as the *Globe and Mail Report* and the *Financial Post*. The database covers all aspects of Canadian business and provides insights into the Canadian perspective on world business activities.

CATFAX: Directory of Mail Order Catalogs (New York: Grey House Publishing, Inc.). 4,000 citations, current

This database indentifies sources for a wide variety of products available through the mails. Records identify the name and address of suppliers, products offered, and sale conditions.

Chemical Industry Notes (Columbus, OH: Chemical Abstracts Service). 450,000 citations, 1974–

Over seventy-five business-oriented periodicals are extracted for this file, which covers all aspects of the chemical processing industry.

Commerce Business Daily (Chicago, IL: U.S. Dept. of Commerce). 120,000 citations, 1982–

This database, updated daily, is the full-text equivalent of the U.S. government publication that announces the proposed procurement by federal agencies of products and services and the awards of contracts by civilian and military agencies of the government. In addition, the file contains occasional references to business-related meetings, to non-U.S. exports, and to other information of interest to U.S. businessmen.

Comprehensive Dissertation Index. (Ann Arbor, MI: University Microfilm International, Inc.). 820,000 citations, 1861–

Based on the work appearing in *Dissertation Abstracts International* and its precursors, Comprehensive Dissertation Index contains citations to the dissertations required for doctoral degrees. The time period covered extends from 1861, when the first academic doctorate was awarded in the United States, to the present. Almost all U.S. dissertations are included, and the number of foreign dissertations is growing steadily. Subject access is principally through the title of the work and a descriptor added for the field in which the work was done. One can search also by name, institution, degree, and year. None of the records contains an abstract, although a citation to *Dissertation Abstracts International* is provided for those dissertations listed in that work.

Disclosure II (Bethesda, MD: Disclosure, Inc.). 9,000 citations, current

This file consists of extracts from official reports issued by companies who must file with the U.S. Securities and Exchange Commission. Information comes from 10-K, 10-Q, 8-K, and 20-F reports along with proxy statements, management discussions, and registration statements on file in the SEC offices. Records in this file tend to be very long, providing full information, rather than merely citations to source documents. One can expect to find significant overlap in information between this file and the PTS Annual Reports Abstracts database.

Dow Jones News (Princeton, NJ: Dow Jones & Company, Inc.). 120,000 references, 1979–

An up-to-date resource for current business news, the Dow Jones News database contains articles appearing in the *Wall Street Journal* and *Barron's* and items disseminated on the Dow Jones News Wire Services.

Duns Market Identifiers 10+ (Parsippany, NJ: Dun's Marketing Services). 1,192,000 records, current

U.S. businesses with at least ten employees are described in this database. Information in the records includes number of employees, address of the company, product line descriptions, financial and marketing data, and corporate affiliations. Over 1,000,000 companies of all types, both public and private, are described.

Electronic Yellow Pages (Westport, CT: Market Data Retrieval, Inc.). 8,500,000 records, current

Electronic Yellow Pages is a set of massive databases providing enhanced access to the type of information available in some 4,800 telephone directories and specialized trade and professional directories throughout the United States. The databases constituting the Electronic Yellow Pages are divided into the following areas: Construction, Financial Services, Manufacturers, Professionals, Retailers, Services, and Wholesalers. Entries in the file provide current names, addresses, and telephone numbers. In addition, certain other information may be provided in some of the subfiles. For example, in the Financial Services Directory, one may search for the size of a firm's assets or the number of people in the city it serves, while in the Professionals Directory, one may search for individuals or for all persons affiliated with specific professional firms. All of the files provide access by four-digit Standard Industrial Classification code (SIC).

EIS Industrial Plants (New York: Economic Information Systems, Inc.). 150,000 records, current

This nonbibliographic database provides access to information about the performance of over 150,000 industrial concerns operated by nearly 70,000 companies whose annual sales total over $500,000. Information in the file is garnered from U.S. government publications, periodical literature, and corporate reports, and directly from the companies themselves.

EIS Nonmanufacturing Establishments (New York: Economic Information Systems, Inc.). 300,000 records, current

Some 250,000 nonmanufacturing concerns employing at least 20 persons are described in this companion to the EIS Industrial Plants database. For each firm one can find current address, number of employees, market share, and other such types of information as it is reported in trade publications, corporate reports, and government publications.

FIND/SVP Reports and Studies Index (New York: FIND/SVP). 7,500 citations, 1977–

The in-depth industry studies and market analyses undertaken by market research firms and investment houses are indexed and abstracted for this database. The output of over 300 sources around the world are included. Indexing provides access to broad industrial groupings and to specific product lines. Records also include purchase prices of individual reports.

FINTEL Newsbase (London: Financial Times Business Information, Ltd., and Predicasts, Inc. [Cleveland OH]). 80,000 citations, 1981–

The online index to the *Financial Times of London*, FINTEL provides access to information about companies, products, and people in business around the world. In addition, the file provides general subject indexing for financial and economic reportage.

Foreign Traders Index (FTI) (Washington, D.C.: U.S. Dept. of Commerce, Trade Facilitation Information and Services Division). 140,000 records, last five years

FTI is a directory of firms and organizations which are known to import goods from the United States or have expressed interest in representing U.S. firms abroad. Records in the file describe the capabilities and the services offered by each of these firms. Access to the file online is presently restricted to U.S. users only.

Frost & Sullivan (New York: Frost & Sullivan, Inc.). 700 citations, 1978–

This database provides descriptions of the detailed market research reports prepared by Frost and Sullivan, Inc. Each record contains a substantial abstract of the report and indexing for each product or line of business discussed in the publication. Since virtually all the Frost and Sullivan reports indexed here are aimed at decision makers in business, access to the sources retrievable in the file will be very limited for users in the general public.

HARFAX Industry Data Sources (Cambridge, MA: HARFAX Database Publishing). 35,000 citations, 1979–

The database describes published sources of financial and marketing statistics for sixty-five major industries of the world. Source materials include major market research studies, assessments of financial institutions, special journal issues, other databases, etc. Access points include Standard Industrial Classification codes, subjects and data descriptors, and geographic designators.

Harvard Business Review (New York: John Wiley & Sons, Inc.). 2,000 records, 1971–

Going beyond mere bibliographic citations, the *Harvard Business Review*'s database contains the full text of articles appearing in the journal since 1977. For 1971 through 1976 the file provides citations and abstracts of *HBR* articles. Subject matter encompasses all areas of business and management thought.

Insurance Abstracts (Ann Arbor, MI: University Microfilms International, Inc.). 60,000 citations, 1979–

References appearing in *Life Insurance Abstracts* and *Property and Liability Index* are concentrated in this file, which covers all aspects of insurance research and practice. In addition to purely business aspects of the field, the database can prove useful as a source of information on topics such as accident prevention and safety education.

LABORDOC (Geneva, Switzerland: International Labour Organization). 100,000 citations, 1965–

The ILO's *International Labour Documentation* in computerized form, this database provides access to all aspects of labor and labor relations. Subjects covered range from articles on industrial relations and work training to monographic works on labor law and environmental issues relating to the life at work.

Management and Marketing Abstracts (MMA) (Leatherhead, England: The Research Association for the Paper and Board, Printing and Packaging Industries). 18,000 citations, 1976–

Both theoretical and practical literature from over 100 international journals is included in the MMA file. The database covers subjects of particular interest to executives and other decision makers functioning in various areas of management and marketing.

Management Contents (Northbrook, IL: Management Contents). 150,000 citations, 1974–

Over 400 international periodicals are indexed and abstracted cover-to-cover in the file. Subject coverage extends to all areas of business operations, decision making, administration, organizational behavior, and public policy. Indexing terminology is drawn from a brief thesaurus maintained and published by the database producer. Significant overlap with the ABI/INFORM database can be expected.

Million Dollar Directory (Parsippany, NJ: Dun's Marketing Services). 125,000 records, current

A comprehensive directory of the largest companies in the United States, this database and its printed equivalents of the same name provide information about sales, number of employees, and lines of business of public and private firms with a net worth of at least $500,000. Entries in the file also include the address and telephone number of the firm and the names of the company's top executives.

NEXIS (Dayton, OH: Mead Data Central and others). 5,000,000 records, time coverage varies (mostly from mid-1970s)

This database is unique in that it contains the full text of a wide range of newspapers and periodicals, allowing users to query much larger bodies of text than is typical in most machine-readable files, which are based on citations or abstracts. A half dozen newspapers, over a dozen business and news magazines, and numerous newsletters and releases from the major wire services are contained in the file. Illustrative of the resources available in NEXIS are: *Christian Science Monitor, Aviation Week & Space Technology, Newsweek, Defense & Foreign Affairs Daily,* and the United Press International's world, national, business, and sports wire services.

Petroleum / Energy Business News Index (P / E News) (New York: American Petroleum Institute). 210,000 citations, 1975–

P/E News provides comprehensive indexing of twelve leading publications in the petroleum and energy field. All editorial matter appearing in publications such as *Platts Oilgram News Service, Middle East Economic Survey,* and the *Lundberg Letter* are included in the file, which is prepared by the American Petroleum Institute's Central Abstracting and Indexing Service.

PTS Annual Reports Abstracts (Cleveland, OH: Predicasts, Inc.). 30,000 records, current

Financial and management information gleaned from the official reports of over 3,000 publicly held companies in the United States is the basis of this database. Both summaries from the discursive portions of the reports and tabular statistical information are provided.

PTS F&S Indexes (Cleveland, OH: Predicasts, Inc.). 2,200,000 citations, 1972–

The F&S Indexes provide access to information about worldwide business developments as reported in trade journals, general business periodicals, and leading newspapers such as the *Wall Street Journal.* In-depth indexing allows the user to retrieve information by company name, by country, by product or line of business, and by activity. The coding for product lines and business activity are quite detailed; in some instances up to a seven-digit Standard Industrial Classification (SIC) code is employed—each modified by an "event" designator such as "New plant and equipment" or "Shipments." The concept of SIC's is expanded by the index producer to allow searching on social, economic, and political aspects of business as well. The database also contains the Predicasts *Source Index*, a directory of all 5,000 publications scanned for the many Predicasts publications.

PTS PROMT (Predicasts Overview of Markets and Technology) (Cleveland, OH: Predicasts, Inc.). 600,000 citations, 1972–

Thousands of business magazines and newspapers as well as government reports and newsletters are scanned for information about international developments relating to the production and marketing of goods and services in the chemical, electronics, metals, paper, plastics, and rubber industries. Detailed abstracts are provided in the file along with statistical summaries. The file can be searched with considerable precision by Standard Industrial Classification (SIC) code plus codes for business "events" and geographic regions.

Standard & Poor's News (New York: Standard & Poor's Corporation). 250,000 records, 1979–

Late-breaking news about more than 10,000 public companies in the United States is summarized in this database, the equivalent of the printed *Daily News* and *Cumulative News* sections of *Standard & Poor's Corporation Records* service. The file reports information such as interim earnings, merger and acquisition news, changes in management, litigation, etc. This file is the archival record for information that is originally entered into the companion file, Standard & Poor's Daily News.

Trade and Industry Index (Menlo Park, CA: Information Access Co.). 350,000 citations, 1981–

Nearly 1,500 business magazines, trade journals, and newspapers such as the *Wall Street Journal* and the *New York Times* are indexed and selectively abstracted in T&I Index. Some 275 sources are indexed cover to cover, and the remainder are scanned selectively for information on new developments in the business world. All lines of business are covered as well as articles on the relationship of business to government and society. The most recent information relevant to this database first appears in the file NEWSEARCH, from which it receives citations on a monthly basis. There will be substantial overlap between this file and

ABI/INFORM, Management Contents, and those of Predicasts, Inc.

Trade Opportunities (Washington, D.C.: Dept. of Commerce, Trade Opportunities Program). 120,000 records, 1976–

Opportunities for U.S. businesses to enter foreign markets are described in this file created from information gathered by the U.S. Department of Commerce. Information includes export opportunities, interest in goods and services that have been expressed by governments and businesses in over 120 countries, data on direct sales leads, and opportunities for U.S. companies to represent foreign concerns in this country. The file is searchable by country, Standard Industrial Classification (SIC) code, and indexing terms. This database is the archival record; the most recent quarter of information appears first in the companion file, Trade Opportunities Weekly. Access to the file is currently restricted to United States users.

U.S. Exports (Washington, D.C.: U.S. Census Bureau, Foreign Trade Division). 400,000 records, 1978–

Statistical information on all commodities exported from the United States to foreign countries is searchable in this file. Information is gathered from official copies of Shipper's Export Declarations. Records provide both dollar values and shipping weights of the goods being exported.

7
Humanities, the Arts, and Architecture

Characteristics and Terminology

The nature of scholarship in the humanities plus the economics of research in the specific disciplines of the field—largely conducted with little or no financial assistance—have contributed to the relatively small number of databases available to assist scholars. When compared to scientific and technical disciplines over the past two decades, the humanities have had little money with which to develop and use computerized information resources. There has simply not been for the humanities the equivalent of a National Technical Information Service or an American Chemical Society or a National Library of Medicine to build and market large and comprehensive databases. But perhaps more significant among the various factors retarding the development of databases for humanities scholarship have been the scholars themselves. Those conducting research in music, art, philosophy, linguistics, and literature have—perhaps from an innate antipathy to machines—been slow to embrace the computer as an aid to research in general and to library research in particular. Their own antipathies aside, however, humanities scholars approach their work in ways significantly different from their colleagues in the sciences.

The goal of research in the natural and the social sciences is the discovery of truth in the form of facts that illuminate or explain specific theories or paradigms. Within the theoretical and experimental framework of a given discipline, scientists build on each other's work, with individuals and research groups adding their own pieces to the ultimate solution of the problem. In the humanities, however, the evolutionary approach to knowledge is less common, and relatively greater importance is placed on individual insights into long-standing problems or the knowledge that comes from new juxtapositions of ideas and images.

While scientific research tends to be additive or evolutionary, humanities research tends to be holistic or cumulative. In science, problems are solved and their solutions quickly become the commonplace building blocks of future inquiries. "Solutions" in the scientific sense are fundamentally meaningless for much of humanities scholarship. The fact that a scholar in Great Britain, for example, has just published a volume on Milton's understanding of Italian painting rarely invalidates or makes less valuable similar work by other Milton scholars. It may be useful to characterize humanistic research in terms of a great landscape with individual works by scholars in the field as aspects of that scene. All contribute to the overall effect, and some pieces may achieve stature as major landmarks, but one element does not necessarily support, in a structural sense, anything else.

The implications of the two approaches to inquiry, the scientific versus the humanistic, are profound when one considers the role of previously published scholarship in the conduct of these very different types of research. The importance of journal literature is significantly greater in the natural sciences than it is in the humanities. Because of the additive nature of research in the scientific disciplines, the problems for investigation are typically defined in such a way that article- or report-length publications can adequately discuss findings. Because the work does tend to be additive, the increased speed of publication available to shorter pieces provides additional incentives for researchers to publish in this form. Humanities scholars, on the other hand, tend to argue their positions in longer forms, assured that their work will continue to have value despite the longer publication schedule such forms usually require.

Regardless of the length of the published piece of scholarship, the use to which the work is put—and by extension, the reason for conducting a literature review to discover it—varies greatly between the scientist and the humanist. For both there is the need to verify that the proposed research has not already been done, but beyond that point the two diverge sharply. Scientists look to the literature for other work that may aid in refining their methodology or that may expedite their own research; that is, they are looking for foundation stones on which they might build. Humanities scholars, in contrast, rely on previous scholarship for discoveries of facts from original sources, for additional support of their own critical insights, or very often for reference points against which to contrast their own ideas. And, at least in the case of literary research, earlier scholarship may itself become an object of literary analysis in its own right; witness, for example, the critical attention devoted to the body of scholarship by one such as T.S. Eliot.

For many scientific disciplines, the useful life of a publication is relatively short, perhaps as little as five years. Eugene Garfield has estimated that in fields such as physics or chemistry, over 60 per cent of the material currently being cited has been published within the last five years. The figure for publications in the arts and humanities offers a dramatic contrast; for example, only 38 per cent of all the articles published in the journal *History* that had been cited recently had come from issues of the past five years.[1] Garfield further notes that in a study of the most heavily cited authors during 1972–1978 conducted by the Institute for Scientific Information, the oldest person in the list for scientific journals was born in 1899, indicating heavy emphasis on current work. In the humanities, the list of the hundred most heavily cited authors included figures such as Homer (9th century, BC) and fully 68 percent were born before 1900. Clearly the time line for humanities is very long.

These very different approaches to research in the canons of earlier investigations has a dramatic effect on the needs for library resources. While the natural scientist will most often need tools that speed access to a body of current scientific papers, a colleague in the humanities will need longer runs of bibliographic tools covering not only journal literature but also monographs and collected works. For traditional library research efforts, the needs of humanities scholars are usually best served by "well-aged" collections, those in which both research aids such as indexes or printed bibliographies and the source materials themselves cover many decades. Whether literally or figuratively, the image of the scholar working quietly among long, musty ranges of volumes has substantial validity.

Because of its highly individualistic, sometimes idiosyncratic nature, humanities literature is often difficult to control through secondary tools. Many of the major finding aids in the humanities are organized around principles that do not always insure easy and precise retrieval. Frequently, they are organized around personalities—authors, artists, composers—or around specific works—*Paradise Lost,* "The Night Watch," "The Rites of Spring," etc. Such an organizing principle is certainly justifiable, but it can provide only a rough segmentation of the literature, particularly where the secondary literature is voluminous. Consider, for example, a tool such as the Modern Language Association's *International Bibliography* which, after first organizing materials by national literature and major time periods, presents entries broken down no more finely than by the author treated. The reader interested in previous scholarship on the character of Bottom in Shakespeare's *A Midsummer Night's Dream* is, thus, confronted with literally pages of articles on Shakespeare and his works. With bibliographic research tools such as this, the scholar finds himself still having to sift through volumes of material in order to find a few bits of needed information. Humanities scholars, therefore, have come to realize that serendipity plays a significant role in their research. It is difficult, indeed, to profile a bibliographic search to retrieve useful articles serendipitously, but progress is being made in the development of databases that can provide assistance in some areas of humanities inquiry.

Although the number of files specifically devoted to humanities research is small—no more than a half dozen or so by the early 1980s—there are at least that many more multidisciplinary databases with substantial coverage of humanities literature. Scholars pursuing research in art, philosophy, or letters also need to bear in mind that such unlikely sounding sources as business, computer science, or agriculture databases may contain many useful references. The AGRICOLA database, for example, has no less than several dozen references on art, music, and folklore relating to agriculture and the rural life, while a file such as ABI/INFORM will be a valuable resources for inquiry into "public art" and the relationships between the corporate and the artistic communities. Ethical and philosophical questions are, of course, significant in all professions, and the databases that serve them contain useful literature. So, as humanities scholars must be able to move among printed bibliographic tools of many academic disciplines, so must they be aware of databases and online searching techniques appropriate not only for files specific to humanities research but also for those in related fields.

Searching for literature in the fields of art, music, philosophy, language, and letters with a computer poses a number of challenges to the scholar. Among the most perplexing of these challenges is the nature of language used in professional communications in the humanities. The vocabulary of philosophical, artistic, and literary discourse is often characterized by common words charged with special meanings. Take, for example, the word "reflection," a term with a commonly understood meaning and used in normal communication in any of a number of contexts. In a philosophical or theological context, however, "reflection" is used—in addition to its common meanings—to denote a very specific mental and/or spiritual exercise. A searcher, then, who needs to search for literature on a topic such as the role of reflection in the teachings of the early Christian church may be hard put to avoid retrieving numerous papers where the word is used without the specialized meaning desired, as for instance, in the sentence, "St. Paul's biases against women can be seen as a reflection of a widely held attitude within the culture from which he came." Because the search system operates on single words or short phrases that can be linked only with rather crude logical connectors, any ambiguity in key terms may significantly reduce the quality of the search product. The problem is both semantic and syntactic.

Contextual cues frequently must be relied upon to convey an author's precise meaning. For a reader who is looking at a printed page, taking in large groups of words and phrases at a time, the task of determining relevance is not nearly so difficult as it is for the person using a computer search system to scan the literature. Syntax plays such a significant role in determining meaning in English that the search analyst must constantly balance the need to create profiles flexible enough to allow variant placements of keywords in a citation against the desire for a profile sufficiently structured so as to minimize irrelevancy.

Related to the problems of pure semantics and syntax is that of style, particularly as it is reflected in the construction of titles for scholarly papers. The literary metaphor is a powerful means of communicating many levels of meaning in a brief verbal image. It is understandably the stock in trade of authors, poets, and dramatists. Because of its power to evoke great meaning with few words, it is often used by scholars in the titles of their own works. On the printed page, and seen in the context of the entire bibliographic citation, a metaphorical title such as "Slouching Toward Bethlehem: WBY and the Rebirth of Irish Letters," can be particularly effective. Not only does it arrest the reader's eye, and quickly establish an allusive connection to the literary artist's (William Butler Yeats) work, but it may also aptly express a good deal about the scholar's own thesis. Unfortunately, it may also be the perpetual source of frustration to the person at the computer terminal. Although the use of allusive titles may be somewhat more prevalent—and therefore more of a problem—in literary research, it is certainly not uncommon in the titles of papers in other fields of the humanities.

Profiling Assistance

While those in the natural and social sciences can frequently rely on published thesauri to help them construct computer profiles, few purely vocabulary-control works exist for the scholar of literature, art, and music. Given the individualistic nature of humanities scholarship, the dearth of subject term lists is understandable, but it leaves one little comfort when faced with the need to structure a search profile. The tools and techniques described here may, at least, provide some means of improving the process of generating search terms.

Cumulative Indexes and Bibliographies.

Lacking a published thesaurus, scholars may find perusal of cumulative indexes or substantial bibliographies a useful method of determining terminological variations in published literature pertinent to their interest. By scanning a printed bibliography or an annual cumulation of a tool like *Humanities Index* or the Modern Language Association's *International Bibliography,* the researcher could be alerted to any commonly established subject headings, to the various ways particular themes are addressed (or alluded to) in titles of secondary works, and to any peculiarities that may exist in references to personal names or titles of works. To take two specific examples, a quick look in *Humanities Index* would remind the researcher in theology or philosophy that references to Saint Paul might refer to him as "Saint Paul," "St. Paul," "Paul" or in the adjectival form "Pauline." For the Spenserian scholar, time spent in this effort would point out that scholarship on *The Faerie Queene* may cite the full name of the classic work, but it may also refer to it either as "FQ" or through some oblique reference to a central character or event in the work, as in the title, "Iconography of Una's Lamb."

This approach will by no means guarantee that all possible methods of referring to authors and artists and their work have been discovered. It will, however, help avoid missing significant references simply through overlooking commonly used terms.

The researcher in the humanities must also consider the possibility of including in a profile an approach that will encompass a broader range of materials than the specific works being studied. For instance, the musicologist doing research on Mozart's "Flute Concerto in G" (K313) will want to put in the terms necessary to retrieve publications specifically mentioning that work. But consideration must also be given to the fact that in the humanities works are often treated collectively. Thus, much relevant information on the "Flute Concerto in G" might very well be found in a paper discussing Mozart's other works for flute or, for that matter, his other works for wind ensembles. The effort required to scan the results of a more general search such as the one suggested for the flute concerto must, of course, be weighed against the need for completeness of retrieval.

Published Reference Tools.

In addition to cumulative volumes of indexes and published bibliographies, there are a variety of other publications that may prove useful for structuring search profiles. Subject-oriented encyclopedias and handbooks exist for each of the major humanities disciplines, and although not numerous, there are a few published thesauri available for consultation. The titles described here are offered as good examples of a larger group of potential search aids.

- *Philosopher's Index Thesaurus,* compiled by Richard H. Lineback (Bowling Green, OH: Philosophy Documentation Center, 1979). Lineback's guide provides the searcher a list of descriptors and cross references used by indexers in the preparation of the printed issues of *Philosopher's Index,* a discussion of the policies and practices followed by indexers in assigning descriptors, and some guidelines useful for searching the database in an online environment.

- *Library of Congress Subject Headings,* 9th ed. with supplements (Washington, D.C.: Government Printing Office, 1980). The standard followed by most academic and research libraries for cataloging their collections, *LCSH* provides thousands of subject headings and related cross references for all fields of inquiry. While only a few databases will actually use Library of Congress subject headings in their records, the *LCSH* can serve as a useful spur to the imagination, particularly when one is having difficulty in determining likely broader terminology for a search profile. In searching those large bibliographic files based on cataloging records of the Library of Congress (e.g. LC/LINE, REMARC, etc.) one will, of course, find not only *LCSH* but also a fairly detailed outline of the Library of Congress classification schedules for call numbers to be invaluable since in those databases one can search both by subject headings, subheadings, and by general classification numbers.

- *The Language of Twentieth Century Music,* by Robert Fink and Robert Ricci (New York: Schirmer, 1975). Besides being a good general dictionary for the study of music in the twentieth century, this volume has a particularly useful appendix grouping topically all the terms defined in the main portion of the text. Thus, under the major heading "Art Movements," one finds terms such as "fauvism," "tachism," etc., or under the heading "Twelve tone music and set theory," the terms "combinatoriality" and "tetrachord."

- *Library of Congress Subject Headings for Recordings of Western Non-Classical Music,* by Judith Kaufman (Philadelphia: Music Library Association, 1983) (MLA Technical Report 14). This volume, aimed principally toward the music cataloger, provides numerous categorized lists of subject headings that have been used by the Library of Congress for recordings of nonclassical music such as jazz, folk music and songs, dance music. Included in the lists are also headings for topical music, such as whaling songs or protest songs.
- *The New Grove Dictionary of Music and Musicians,* edited by Stanley Sadie (London: Macmillan, 1980). This massive set, long a standard work in music research and now extending to twenty volumes, provides informed discussion of virtually every aspect of musical theory, composition, performance, and history. It can provide not only a respectable overview of most questions related to music, but also good clues to terminology and other pieces of information useful to a search for music-related topics. For research in areas of folk and non-Western music, an appendix in volume 20 will prove most useful as it provides a glossary of terms.
- *Encyclopedia of World Art* (New York: McGraw-Hill, 1968). This fifteen-volume set covers art and architecture throughout history. It's volume-long index can prove particularly valuable in selecting search terms for specific works, artistic techniques, aesthetic principles, and other topics related to art throughout history.

Databases

As has already been pointed out in this chapter, the number of databases directly covering the disciplines of the humanities and the fine arts is quite small. Much material of value to a scholarly inquiry in the humanities will be found in other resources, aimed at a different audience such as psychologists, business professionals, or anthropologists. Consequently, the humanities scholar will be well advised to explore the database descriptions in other sections of this book, particularly those in the social sciences.

ARTBIBLIOGRAPHIES MODERN (Santa Barbara, CA: ABC-CLIO, Inc.). 70,000 citations, 1974–

Secondary literature in the form of books, dissertations, and periodical articles plus exhibition catalogs are included in this database. Coverage encompasses artistic endeavors of the nineteenth and twentieth centuries. All media are covered, from painting and sculpture to ceramics and printing, and more general articles on art history and biography are included as well.

Avery Index (New York, Columbia University, Avery Library). 6,200 citations, 1980–

A continuation of the well-known *Avery Index to Architectural Periodicals,* this file contains the indexing records prepared by the staff of the Avery Architectural and Fine Arts Library of Columbia University. Over 350 art and architecture periodicals are scanned for materials to go into the database. Indexing conforms generally with the headings used by the Library of Congress, but many additional headings have been created in order to provide better access to the research specific to the field of architecture. Records in the file are bibliographic in nature, that is, abstracts are not prepared.

BIOETHICSLINE (Washington, D.C.: Georgetown University, Kennedy Center for Bioethics). 13,000 citations, 1973–

The annual *Bibliography of Bioethics* in computer form, BIOETHICSLINE draws from a number of other indexing resources, several databases, and nearly 100 additional journals. It covers the wide range of philosophical, moral, and ethical issues confronting medical professionals and policymakers today. Topics searchable in the file range from research problems utilizing recombinant DNA to genetic counseling, from euthanasia to the refusal of lifesaving treatment based on religious beliefs.

Comprehensive Dissertation Index (Ann Arbor, MI: University Microfilms International, Inc.). 820,000 citations, 1861–

Based on the work appearing in *Dissertation Abstracts International* and its precursors, Comprehensive Dissertation Index contains citations to the dissertations required for doctoral degrees. The time period covered extends from 1861, when the first academic doctorate was awarded in the United States, to the present. Almost all U.S. dissertations are included, and the number of foreign dissertations is growing steadily. Subject access is principally through the title of the work and a descriptor added for the field in which the work was done. One can search also by name, institution, degree, and year. None of the records contain abstracts, although a citation to *Dissertation Abstracts International* is provided for those dissertations listed in that work.

Eighteenth Century Short Title Catalog (London: The British Library Reference Division). 137,000 citations

A joint project of the British Library and the North American Center for The Eighteenth-Century Short Title Catalogue (ESTC/NA), this database contains records of English-language items published in Britain or its colonies during the eighteenth century. Records include basic publishing information and descriptive notes of the publication plus notations regarding libraries that have reported ownership.

Journal of the Society of Architectural Historians (JSAH) (Philadelphia, PA: Society of Architectural Historians). 1,600 citations, 1941–

The JSAH database includes abstracts of articles appearing in the *Journal of the Society of Architectural Historians* plus citations to reviews of books and exhibits appearing in that publication. Subjects represented in the file include architectural and art history, landscape architecture, aesthetics, and related topics.

Language and Language Behavior Abstracts (LLBA) (San Diego, CA: Sociological Abstracts, Inc.). 70,000 citations, 1973–

Corresponding to the printed abstracting service of the same name, the LLBA database provides coverage of international journal literature on language, its development, and use in both its written and spoken forms. Coverage extends to areas such as speech behavior and therapy, nonverbal communication, and various specialties of linguistics and textual analysis.

LC/LINE See MACHINE READABLE CATALOGING (MARC)

LC/MARC. See MACHINE READABLE CATALOGING (MARC)

Machine Readable Cataloging (MARC) (Washington, D.C.: Library of Congress). 1,000,000 citations, 1968–

This file contains complete bibliographic records from the Machine Readable Cataloging (MARC) program of the Library of Congress. English-language materials since 1968 and non-English materials from varying dates since that time are included. The file can be searched by author, title, and subject as well as by a number of other access points, such as imprint date and publisher. All subject fields are represented, but the file should be of particular value to researchers in book-oriented disciplines such as the humanities and the social sciences.

Modern Language Association Bibliography (New York: Modern Language Association of America). 469,000 citations, 1970–

The machine-readable equivalent of the Modern Language Association's *International Bibliography,* this file consists of citations from hundreds of journals and essay collections in the area of language and literature. Subject scope for the file includes theoretical and applied linguistics, folklore, foreign language teaching, and studies of American, English, Celtic, Latin, European, Asian, African, and Latin American literatures. Indexing terminology is minimal in database records, so searchers must rely heavily on titles to provide search keys. The database does contain a coding scheme that provides a convenient method of selecting large national and chronological groups, e.g., English literature of the nineteenth century.

Philosopher's Index (Bowling Green, OH: Bowling Green State University, Philosophy Documentation Center). 100,000 citations, 1940–

Books and nearly 300 journals covering all areas of philosophical inquiry are abstracted in this database. In addition to publications on aesthetics, ethics, metaphysics, and other fundamental aspects of philosophy as an academic discipline, the file extends to works discussing philosophical dimensions of other fields, such as medicine, law, education, and science. Indexing terms for the file are now drawn from the *Philosopher's Index Thesaurus* by Richard Lineback.

REMARC (Arlington, VA: Carrollton Press, Inc.). 770,000 citations, pre–1980

The REMARC (Retrospective MARC) database cuts across all disciplinary lines. It contains cataloging records for materials appearing in the Library of Congress shelflist prior to 1968 for English-language materials and with somewhat later dates for non-English items. The file represents the bulk of materials cataloged by the Library of Congress prior to the advent of the computer-assisted systems for library cataloging now in use today. Searches may be conducted not only on traditional access points such as author and title but also on words in subject headings, imprint dates, publishers, etc. For cataloged works since the beginning of the Machine Readable Cataloging (MARC) program at the Library of Congress, one should consult the MARC database.

RILM (New York, City University of New York, International RILM Center). 44,000 citations, 1972–

Corresponding to the publication, *RILM (Répertoire International de Littérature Musicale) Abstracts,* this database provides comprehensive coverage of music-related literature. Citations include publications on musicians, music theory and performance, musicology, and instruments plus literature on related areas such as philosophy, psychology, and acoustics. Sources covered are international in their scope.

Notes

1. Eugene Garfield. "Is Information Retrieval in the Arts and Humanities Inherently Different from That in Science? The Effect that ISI's Citation Index for the Arts and Humanities Is Expected to Have on Future Scholarship." *Library Quarterly* 20, 1(1980):40–57.

8
Legal Research

Characteristics and Terminology

In the days of Thomas Jefferson, a young man aspiring to the practice of law followed what was by then a long-established method of training drawn from the English tradition. He attached himself to an established attorney and "read the law" until such time as he could gain admittance to the bar. The "law" that the legal apprentice read was typically contained in a relatively small number of volumes, usually treatises, such as those by Blackstone or Coke, on major topics. Having served an apprenticeship and been admitted to the bar, the new lawyer might very well conduct a respectable practice with no more books than he could carry. He would have had little opportunity to call upon the vast resources of libraries, legal or otherwise, if indeed such resources had even been available. The nature of legal training and practice continued without substantial change until well past the mid-nineteenth century, when modern, university-based law schools were born.

The Industrial Revolution and the dramatic changes that have evolved over the past century in the role of government in the private lives of citizens have substantially changed the nature of legal practice. In the English-speaking world, the common law concept of precedent as manifest in the doctrine of *stare decisis* has long held sway, so that much of the law governing daily conduct must be found through the skillful matching of present fact with past decisions. In a world of slow changes the body of literature and the sources necessary for legal research were quite manageable. The rapid growth of industrial societies and the technological revolutions so intimately connected with them created situations for which the courts had no precedents or for which the application of old remedies would result in grave injustices. Consequently, the role of statutory and other forms of law began to increase, thereby greatly complicating the task of the legal practitioner.

Today's legal structure and the society in which it operates are highly complex, requiring that attorneys be able to locate quickly pertinent statutory, regulatory, and case law in a broad range of fields. Indeed, cases today may require of the attorney sophisticated knowledge in technology, basic science, psychology, economics, or a host of other disciplines. Merely keeping abreast of legal issues today is difficult; mastery of them—in the sense that Thomas Jefferson might have known "the Law"—is virtually impossible. The resources of a good-sized law collection with copies of relevant codes, case reporters, loose-leaf updating services, and other supporting publications is essential for most practitioners in the 1980s.

As the bulk of law publications has grown to enormous proportions over the years, so too has the need for research aids in the form of indexes, citations, and digests. Legal research problems may entail matching the conditions of a current case with previous facts, with specific juristic concepts, or with specific statutes, regulations, or administrative edicts. In order to accomplish this task, the researcher needs tools providing many access points. The tools that have been developed to meet these needs are often wonderfully ingenious—although often dismayingly complex to the uninitiated.

The access tools for legal research are of two types: those providing access to the body of law itself and other publications providing coverage of secondary legal literature (journal articles, etc.). The tools for accessing the law itself consist mainly of the indexes accompanying statutory or case compilations, of large multi-volume digests (e.g., *West's Federal Practice Digest, 2d*), and citators (indexes to cases, statutes, and rulings that have been cited in court decisions). One could also include in this group of tools the many loose-leaf services that cover large areas of legal practice, such as taxation, federal regulation of specific industries, and labor relations. The collateral research tools consist largely of treatises on such topics as contracts and of various indexing or abstracting services covering articles in law journals and other publications in supporting fields. Depending on the topic under investigation, the tool used may be specific to legal resources (e.g., *Legal Periodicals Index*) or it may cover an area of professional practice in another field related to the law (e.g., *Accountants' Index* or *Public Affairs Information Service*).

When moving between these two types of access tools, researchers will need to adjust their searching strategies. The tools for access to the law itself are usually geared to searching for legal concepts, specific facts, or known precedents. Collateral research tools, on the other hand, are very often organized around a more general framework of subjects or utilize terminology derived from professional practice in other fields such as accounting or political science.

Regardless of which kind of tool is used, research on legal issues can tax both the capabilities of access publications and the inventiveness of the legal researcher. Because of the importance attached to precedents, legal researchers very often must consult case literature and legislative histories decades old. To do this job efficiently, they must have indexes and other search tools that cover a long time span. Yet the law is constantly changing, and the world is growing ever more complex through advances in technology and redefinitions of governmental and societal responsibilities. In such a world the attorney and the legal scholar must also be able to find information in fields where the terminology is still evolving or where some concepts are not yet fully defined. Witness, for example, the unsettled state of affairs regarding copyright in relation to home television recorders or the controversies that continue to rage over doctors' responsibilities in a world where it is possible to deliver a healthy child from a mother declared "brain dead" two months previously.

Although the computer cannot replace the judgment required for sound legal and judicial decisions, the bibliographic files in supporting fields and legal research systems that have been developed over the past decade offer great hope for easing the burden of the researcher. The development of two online systems in particular—LEXIS and WESTLAW—promise to revolutionize the nature of research in statutory, regulatory, and case law. Both LEXIS, from Mead Data Central, and WESTLAW, from the West Publishing Company, have been designed to provide the law scholar and the attorney access to the complete text of source documents. Both LEXIS and WESTLAW are systems based on groups or "libraries" of databases covering state and federal laws, federal regulations and administrative rulings, and the decisions of many state and federal courts. The time periods covered by these databases vary, but many of the files extend back to the 1930s and a few even earlier. LEXIS, the stronger of the two in coverage of state statutes and court decisions and in French and British law, uses the terminology of the source documents as the access keys for retrieval. WESTLAW, in contrast, takes advantage of the considerable editorial and indexing refinements provided by West Publishing Company. Files on the WESTLAW system can be searched both by words in the text of the decisions and code sections and by the topic headings and key topic numbers with which the West editors index materials for their many court reporter services such as *Supreme Court Reporter* and *Federal Reporter*.

As the number of databases has grown in virtually all fields over the past ten years, so have the files covering the secondary literature of the law and the loose-leaf services that are so much a part of legal practice. Many of these files reflect the general trend in database production and cover only materials on a current basis or extended back in time only to the late 1960s or early 1970s. These files also differ from WESTLAW and LEXIS in that they provide access only to indexing terminology and abstracts rather than to the full text of the original source materials. The marketing strategies followed by both LEXIS and WESTLAW will make it easy for the legal researcher to access with the same equipment both the major resource (LEXIS or WESTLAW) and the other bibliographic systems such as DIALOG and ORBIT. With the hardware problems associated with accessing multiple database systems solved, it appears likely that legal researchers will find a greater need than ever to develop proficiency in the construction of profiles for computer searching.

Before turning to specific profiling tools, it may be useful to consider the differences in profile construction between files that contain document "surrogates," that is, abstracts or indexed citations, and files that allow searching of the full text of documents. The vast majority of databases now available online are built on records that attempt to represent the content of the original document in a highly abbreviated form. Generally the language of a document "surrogate" can be considered to be more semantically charged than that in the document it describes; that is, word-for-word the terminology in a bibliographic citation and abstract carries more meaning than a passage of the same size in the original text. The indexer and abstracter use language that attempt to translate the author's words into more standardized terminology and to provide the library user a number of access points with which to retrieve the citations at some point in the future. Thesauri, code numbering schemes, and other such tools are among the most commonly used devices for effecting a high degree of retrievability with the conciseness required for brief records. For the library user, and especially for the online searcher, the task of effective retrieval depends largely on the ability to utilize the thesauri and user manuals to "decode" the information locked away in the file. Once mastered, however, these terminology and classification standards can streamline search profiles, making possible the retrieval of highly precise information with a minimum number of keywords and/or classification codes.

Because the indexers and abstracters must, however, capture an author's meaning in a fraction of the original space, they may have to sacrifice—or leave to the reader's deductive abilities—some information provided by the author. For example, it is a common indexing/abstracting practice to focus on results rather than on background issues or methodologies. Users who are interested in methodology may, consequently, be frustrated in their efforts to retrieve relevant material. They may need to construct a profile that retrieves a broader, less precise, group of documents and to edit the resulting bibliography after consulting the original sources for the information they contain about the methods employed.

Full-text databases, in contrast, make the words of the entire document available for searching. While such databases greatly improve the accessibility of the information in the publications, the overall chances for retrieving irrelevant citations are increased. The nature of language in a text of twenty-five pages is inevitably less heavily loaded with terms that carry real meaning than is a

PROBLEM: What information is available regarding water rights?

LOGIC: (WESTLAW)
(WATER RIPARIAN) & RIGHT*

(DIALOG)
SELECT (WATER OR RIPARIAN) AND RIGHT?

RESULTS:		
	FEDERAL REPORTER (1945-)	7065 cases (150 per year)
	LEGAL RESOURCES INDEX (1980-)	156 items (52 per year)
	SOCIAL SCIENCES CITATION INDEX (1972-)	81 items (8 per year)
	NATIONAL TECHNICAL INFORMATION SERVICE (1964-)	1119 items (62 per year)

Figure 8-1. Comparison of search results between a full text file and indexing/abstracting service files.

carefully prepared keyword list or abstract. Profiles for searching such a volume of words must therefore account for relatively greater variations in the ways a concept might be expressed. In searches on legal topics this problem can be acute. Consider, for instance, the many ways a judge might express the concept of contractual obligation—"contractually bound," "a valid contract was established," etc. It is more likely as well that the full text of an article or court decision or other piece of prose will use language metaphorically, which adds little but frustration to the scholar using a highly literal tool such as a computer. The researcher must approach the task of profile construction in full-text files with an extra measure of care in order to avoid linguistic traps. Profiles in full-text files will often need to rely on specific phrases or closely linked terms more heavily than single word combinations. For example, Figure 8-1 shows the results of a broadly formulated search on water rights in four databases—the Federal Reporter of WESTLAW, the Legal Resources Index from Information Access Corporation, the Social Sciences Citation Index from the Institute for Scientific Information, and the NTIS database of the National Technical Information Service. The results clearly indicate that a loosely formulated query used in a full-text database can pull enormous numbers of citations from the file. In this case the quality of the citations is very mixed for the Federal Reporter, retrieving cases in which the words often bear no relation to the concept of "water rights." For example, the results included a case in which "right" was used in a judicial definition of the right or left side of a stream, a number of other instances dealing with the rectitude of actions that led to water pollution, and still others where the issue at hand dealt with seamen's rights in navigable waters. The index and abstracts files yielded far fewer citations per year, largely due to the number of access points provided by the indexing and abstracting records, yet the quality of the results was uniformly high, with virtually every citation directly on target.

With research systems such as WESTLAW the user has the option of relying solely on full-text terms or of using the indexing structures and controlled lists of legal topic headings supplied by West editors in order to focus search results. LEXIS searchers, on the other hand, must rely on the original text alone to provide the necessary clues.

Profiling Assistance

Because legal research can take the attorney or scholar into many fields, the suggestions offered in earlier chapter will provide guidance for searches in databases not wholly devoted to legal issues. For example, for searches on the legal aspects of teacher unions, one may choose to search the Educational Resources Information Center's database (ERIC) for which the *Thesaurus of ERIC Descriptors* would provide assistance. For searches of databases directly related to legal issues, there are a number of resources that one can use for constructing effective online profiles. Illustrative of the tools one may wish to consult are the following:

- *Corpus Juris Secundum*, 106 volumes (St. Paul, MN: West Publishing Co.). A massive, encyclopedic work, *Corpus Juris Secundum* provides the reader not only with terms appropriate for the entire range of legal concepts but also with densely annotated overviews of those concepts as they have evolved.

The annotations can prove doubly useful in that they frequently cite landmark decisions that might be used for tracking down related cases that cited them as precedent.

- Case Digests. The many case-digest services providing subject access to the decisions of state and federal courts can provide profiling help in several ways. The digest subject headings and the abstracts or headnotes are a rich source of terminology. In the case of profiles for WESTLAW, the topic headings and their numerical "key number" equivalents can be searched directly, providing a convenient method of establishing a subject context for a set of search terms. To illustrate, consider the case of a searcher wishing to locate cases in WESTLAW dealing with the question of the conditions under which a teacher may be dismissed when there are charges of moral misconduct. With search terms such as "immoral," "moral turpitude," and "sexual" the searcher may choose to match the topic heading "Teachers. Suspension, Removal, and Reassignment. Grounds for Removal or Suspension"—or more briefly, its numeric equivalent 141(4)—as a convenient method of establishing the context for the other search terms. In addition to the core volumes of the digests that contain the headnotes themselves, two other groups of volumes can be especially valuable profiling aids, that is, *Words and Phrases* and the *Descriptive Word Index*. The latter is primarily useful as a guide to the proper topic headings in the core volumes, while the former lists words and phrases that have been judicially defined—a particularly good clue to terms that may prove troublesome in a search. Among the numerous digests available are *Supreme Court Digest* and *West's Federal Practice Digest, 2d*.

- *Black's Law Dictionary* (St. Paul, MN: West Publishing Co., 1979). Long a standard legal reference, *Black's* provides not only concise definitions of and synonyms for legal terms but also other valuable guides to variations (abbreviations, etc.) that are likely to be encountered in legal texts.

- *Legal Thesaurus*, by William C. Burton (New York: Macmillan, 1980). This volume provides lists of synonyms for over

7,600 principal legal terms plus an extensive cross-reference index from individual synonyms back to the main term groups. This tool will be invaluable when searching full-text files such as WESTLAW and LEXIS.

Databases

The databases described here are restricted to those files covering law journals and loose-leaf services or those databases devoted exclusively to regulatory, statutory, or case law. Clearly, a number of other databases, particularly those discussed in Chapter 4 (Social Sciences and Education) will have much of value to legal researchers as well.

Chemical Regulations and Guidelines System (CRGS) (Fairfax, VA: CRC Systems, Inc.). 5,000 citations, current

Regulations and guidelines as well as pertinent federal standards and specifications governing chemicals are covered in this file. In addition to facts related to the regulations themselves, the file provides access by the name of the substance and the CAS registry number. Coverage includes both citations to the *Code of Federal Regulations* and the *Federal Register*.

CHEMLAW (Washington, D.C.: Bureau of National Affairs, Inc., and Fein-Marquart Associates, Inc.). 15,000 citations, current

All aspects of manufacture, use, and disposal of chemical substances are covered in this database, which contains the full text of chemical regulations from the *Code of Federal Regulations* and the *Federal Register* plus references to the Bureau of National Affairs publication *Chemical Regulation Reporter*.

Electronic Legislative Search System (ELSS) (Chicago, IL: Commerce Clearing House, Inc.). 1981

The thousands of bills introduced in Congress and in the legislatures of the fifty states, and the tens of thousands of actions relating to them, are tracked in this database. Users may query the file by state, by subject code, and by specific action or bill status. Updating is continuous so that in many instances one may retrieve information as current as actions of the previous day.

Federal Register Search System (FRSS) (Bethesda, MD: U.S. National Institutes of Health and U.S. Environmental Protection Agency). 100,000 citations, 1978–

This file provides weekly updated information on federal regulations—both proposed and final—related to chemical substances. Records describe the action being proposed by various federal agencies, list significant dates related to the promulgation and/or enforcement of the regulation, and cite the section or sections of the *Code of Federal Regulations* that will be affected by the new or modified regulation.

LABORLAW (Washington, D.C.: Bureau of National Affairs, Inc.). 200,000 citations, 1938–

A combination of several information services from the Bureau of National Affairs, Inc., LABORLAW provides both summaries of decisions and references to published labor-related court opinions. Areas of labor relations, fair employment, wages and hours, and occupational safety and health are included. The entire file and specific subfiles can be searched; the subfiles include *Labor Relations Reporter, Labor Arbitration Reports, Fair Employment Practices Cases, Wage and Hours Cases, Occupational Safety and Health Cases*, and *Mine Safety and Health Cases*. Date coverage varies by subfile.

Legal Resource Index (LRI) (Menlo Park, CA: Information Access Co.). 100,000 citations, 1980–

Nearly 700 law journals and five legal newspapers are indexed intensively in LRI. All editorial matter is indexed, including editorials, case notes, columns, and letters to the editor. These citations are supplemented with references to books, government publications, and articles from general interest magazines and newspapers.

LEXIS (Dayton, OH: Mead Data Central and others)

A massive full-text system, LEXIS contains the complete text of laws, regulations, administrative rulings, and court decisions. The file is organized into numerous sub-databases or "libraries" relating to a specific subject or jurisdiction. Among the libraries available are the following:

General Federal Library, containing the *U.S. Code, Code of Federal Regulations, Federal Register*, and decisions from the Supreme Court, Courts of Appeals, district courts, and the Court of Claims.

Patent, Trademark, and Copyright Library, consisting of federal case law, some back to 1938.

Tax Library, containing the entire Internal Revenue Code, IRS rulings, *Cumulative Bulletin*, and case law, some as early as 1913.

Securities Library, containing relevant *U.S. Code* and *Code of Federal Regulations* information plus court decisions and rulings from the Securities and Exchange Commission.

Trade Regulations Library, containing decisions and rulings from federal courts and the Federal Trade Commission.

Communications Library, containing federal court decisions dating back to 1936 plus volumes 39–42 of *Federal Communications Commission Reports*.

Labor Library, consisting of federal court decisions and determinations by the National Labor Relations Board.

Bankruptcy Library, containing federal court decisions and the rulings of bankruptcy judges.

State Law Libraries, containing for all fifty states and the District of Columbia decisions of lower courts, appellate courts, and courts of last resort. For some states, coverage extends back to 1821.

In addition to U.S. laws and court decisions, LEXIS provides access to major statutory and case law from Great Britain and France. *Shepard's Citations*, a tool allowing the researcher to identify subsequent cases citing an earlier decision, is available on LEXIS as is the text of standard legal publications from Matthew Bender & Company, titles such as Collier's *Bankruptcy*, and several standard forms volumes.

PATLAW (Washington, D.C.: Bureau of National Affairs, Inc.). 15,000 cases, 1967–

The PATLAW database is derived from the *United States Patent Quarterly*, the patent information service of the Bureau of National

Affairs, Inc. While the printed service provides indexing and the full text of patent and trademark decisions, the online file provides only abstracts and bibliographic citations. Subject matter covers all aspects of litigation dealing with patents, trademarks, copyrights, and unfair competition.

WESTLAW (St. Paul, MN: West Publishing Co.)

The WESTLAW system, a collection of statutory and case law databases, provides detailed retrieval of legal materials using indexing terminology, headnote abstracts, and the full text of the source materials. The files can be searched for words or phrases used in administrative or court rulings, federal regulations, U.S. Code statements of law, plus the terminology and coding used by the editors of West Publishing Company in their preparation of materials for publication in tools such as *Supreme Court Reporter, Federal Reporter, Federal Supplement,* and their many state and regional reporters. The major libraries currently available through the WESTLAW system are:

Supreme Court Reporter, 1925–.
Federal Reporter, 2d, 1945–.
Federal Supplement, 1950–.
State and regional reporters, such as South Western Reporter and Atlantic Reporter, varying coverage.
Opinions by state attorneys general for selected states, recent coverage.
Military Justice Reporter
United States Code Annotated
Code of Federal Regulations

Numerous subject-oriented libraries on topics such as bankruptcy, securities, taxation, labor relations, antitrust and business regulation, communications, government contracts, insurance, and education are included as well. In addition, WESTLAW contains *Shepard's Citations,* which provides references to subsequent cases citing an earlier case.

Glossary

BAUD RATE. A standard measure for rating the speed of data communications. For example, a terminal operating at 1200 baud (generally equivalent to 1200 bits-per-second) can send or receive data at roughly 120 characters per second or about 1200 words per minute.

BOOLEAN LOGIC. The logic operations available in computer literature searching resulting from the connectors, OR, AND, and NOT.

COMPUTER TAG. Alphabetic, numeric, or alphanumeric designators that are used in machine-readable records. Tags serve a variety of purposes, ranging from labeling the format of an original source (e.g., article, book, etc.) to their function as codes to direct computer typesetting programs regarding the placement of a citation in a printed index. In online systems, computer tags are often searchable elements in the database, thus providing users additional means to refine the product of online queries.

CONNECT TIME. Refers to the amount of time the searcher's terminal is in physical connection to a host computer system. Charges for computer searching generally include connect time as a major element in the cost equation.

COORDINATE INDEX. A nonhierarchical index based on the matching, or coordination, of individual terms specified by the user at the time of retrieval. It is the principle behind computerized information retrieval systems.

CRT (CATHODE RAY TUBE). Computer jargon for terminals displaying results on a television-like screen. In some literature they are also known as VDUs or Video Display Units.

DATA COMMUNICATIONS NETWORK. Any of a growing number of long distance telecommunications networks providing computer communications at rates lower than normal long distance telephone tolls. Currently the most commonly used such systems in the United States are Tymnet, Telenet, and Uninet.

DATABASE. A collection of information items—facts, observations, bibliographic references, abstracts, etc.—organized for future access. In most of the systems now available for library research a "database" corresponds to all or part of an already existing indexing service such as *Chemical Abstracts.* The database may have more, the same, or less information than its print equivalent, but it almost always is organized for computer searching in such a way as to provide a greater number of access points than the print tool.

DATABASE PRODUCER. The firm or organization that collects original source materials and creates citations or abstracts that are then made available to users. In many instances these firms or organizations are the publishers of printed indexes such as *Chemical Abstracts* or *Engineering Index.* Database producers may also have their own computer searching software for querying the database, but more typically they sell or lease access to their file to third parties called ONLINE VENDORS.

DESCRIPTOR. A vocabulary term or subject heading controlled by the indexing authority used for a database. Descriptors may be single- or multi-word terms that are intended to be applied with consistency by indexers as they prepare references for a DATABASE. Search strategies relying heavily on descriptors are often developed when a high degree of relevance is desired. Because the establishment of widely accepted terminology takes a good deal of time, descriptor lists may not always reflect the latest terms that are being used in a field, hence the need to supplement descriptors with FREE TEXT terminology or IDENTIFIERS.

DOWNLOADING. The practice of collecting online search results in machine-readable rather than printed forms so that the data can be further manipulated or added to the user's own computer files. The growing use of micro-computers as terminals for conducting online literature searches has made downloading possible for users. The ethical and legal issues surrounding downloading are, however, still hotly debated.

END USER. The person for whom a literature search is conducted, as opposed to the intermediary or SEARCH ANALYST who may have actually conducted the search. As computer information systems are made easier for the casual user to manipulate, greater emphasis will appear on searches conducted by end users.

FALSE HIT. A citation retrieved in a computer search that meets the requirements of the stated logic, yet is irrelevant because of semantic or syntactic variations that were either unanticipated in the original profile or were unavoidable.

FREE TEXT. Refers to inquiries of a database in which the searcher requests retrieval from the file based on word combinations without regard to any vocbulary authority list. The resulting citation list would normally then consist of references containing those words if they appeared in the title, the keyword (or DESCRIPTOR) list, or the abstract. Free text searching increases one's chances of finding the greatest absolute number of relevant references, but it also increases the chances of retrieving the greatest number of irrelevant citations.

FULL TEXT. Refers to databases containing the entire text of articles, cases, or other original information sources. These files are distinguished from bibliographic databases, which contain only bibliographic references and perhaps summaries.

IDENTIFIER. A type of keyword added to a bibliographic citation to improve its retrievability. Identifiers differ from DESCRIPTORS in that they are terms usually drawn from the original text and do not conform to a standard vocabulary list. In many databases identifiers are used to highlight either new concepts for which no commonly agreed upon subject terms exist or specific names (e.g., of tests) for which a general subject term has been deemed inappropriate.

INFORMATION UTILITY. An information service providing online access to and perhaps manipulation of a wide variety of information resources. The companies and the services they offer are highly diverse and are evolving steadily. Typical of firms calling themselves information utilities are companies such as The Source and Compuserve, which offer a broad menu of databases and computer programs via telephone dialup systems.

INVERTED INDEX (INVERTED FILE). The computer index containing each access point in a machine-readable record on which a search can be made. Inverted indexes are central to online computer systems, allowing them to search vast numbers of terms without having to scan long strings of textual matter.

KEYWORD. A generic term usually denoting those terms in a bibliographic citation that epitomize the content of the source document. In a narrow sense "keyword" refers to terms in the DESCRIPTOR and IDENTIFIER fields of the citation. More generally, however, the word is used to mean any subject-related terms that might be used in a computer search, regardless of whether those words appear in other fields such as title or abstract.

MODEM. The telecommunications device linking computer terminals and computer systems through telephone circuits. The name derives from the device's function as a *mod*ulator and *dem*odulator of the high pitched tone or carrier signal used by the telephone to carry the messages between data processing equipment. The term is often used as a synonym for acoustic coupler.

OFFLINE. A method of data processing in which all search requirements are processed without interaction between the computer and the user; also referred to as batch mode processing since it is most economical to process large numbers of computer jobs together in this fashion.

ONLINE. A method of processing information in which the user is able to interact with the computer during the searching process, that is, while the equipment is on the line to the computer.

ONLINE VENDOR. The provider of computing services via dial-up networks. Online vendors typically perform two principal tasks. They create and maintain searching system software for use with a number of databases, and they act as intermediaries in acquiring machine-readable files from DATABASE PRODUCERS. In some cases online vendors function as database producers as well.

SEARCH ANALYST. One who, through training, experience, or job responsibility, constructs information search strategies and conducts searches for information using computer retrieval systems. Over the past decade this term has come to be applied to librarians and information specialists who act as intermediaries for searching the large online bibliographic and textual databases made available through systems such as DIALOG, BRS, and ORBIT.

TITLE ENRICHMENT. An indexing technique for improving the information content of an author's title by adding words or phrases to the title. Usually enrichment terms are drawn from the body of the original text and may not conform to a standardized vocabulary list as do DESCRIPTORS.

Index

ABI/INFORM, 95, 124, 129, 139, 143
ABI/INFORM codes, 128
ABI/INFORM Users Guide, 124, 129
Abstract Bulletin of the Institute of Paper Chemistry, 110
Abstracts of Tropical Agriculture, 50
Accountants' Index, 130
Accountants' Index, 155
ADTRACK, 130
Advertising and Marketing Intelligence, 130
AGRICOLA, 25, 27, 31, 36, 39, 143
AGRICOLA Users Guide, 39
AHL. *See* America: History and Life
AIM/ARM, 63
Alcohol Use-Abuse Database, 39
Alloys Index, 94, 108
America: History & Life, 60
America: History & Life (AHL), 64
American Banker, 130
American Men and Women of Science, 95
American Statistics Index, 64
Animal Behavior Abstracts, 46
Animal Breeding Abstracts, 41
APILIT, 95
APIPAT, 96
APTIC, 96
AQUACULTURE, 39
AQUALINE, 39
Aquatic Sciences and Fisheries Abstracts, 40
ARTBIBLIOGRAPHIES MODERN, 149
Avery Index, 149
Avery Index to Architectural Periodicals, 149

Banker, 130
Baud rate, 165
Beilstein, 98
BHRA Fluid Engineering, 96
Bibliographic Retrieval Service, 125
Bibliography of Agriculture, 39
Bibliography of Bioethics, 149
Bibliography and Index of Geology, 95, 104
Bibliography of the History of Medicine, 70
Bibliography on Racism, 72
Bibliography of Vertebrate Paleontology, 104
Bilingual Education Bibliographic Abstracts, 64
BIOETHICSLINE, 149
Biological Abstracts, 23, 40, 50, 61
Biological Abstracts/RRM, 40
Bio-Research Index, 40
BIOSIS Previews, 36, 40, 46
BIOSIS Search Guide, 33, 40

Black's Law Dictionary, 60, 160
BLS Consumer Price Index, 65
BLS Employment, Hours, and Earnings, 65
BLS Labor Force, 65
BLS Producer Price Index, 65
BNF Abstracts, 109
Boolean logic, 165
Business International/Data Forecasts, 130
Business International/Data Time Series, 131

CAB, 41, 46
CAB Online Search Guide, 41
Canadian Business Periodicals Index, 131
Canadian Newspaper Index, 66
Carbon 13 Nuclear Magnetic Resonance Search System, 97
CA Search, 25, 40, 96
CAS Online, 97
CAS registry numbers, 27–30, 40, 42, 48, 50, 82, 89–91, 96–97, 107, 110, 113, 117
CASSI, 97
Catalyst Resource for Women, 66
CATFAX: Directory of Mail Order Catalogs, 131
CESARS. *See* Chemical Evaluation Search and Retrieval System
CHEMDEX, 30, 91
Chemical Abstracts, 6, 42, 50, 61, 89
Chemical Abstracts Index Guide, 29, 31, 90
Chemical Abstracts Source Index, 97
Chemical Engineering Abstracts, 98
Chemical Evaluation Search and Retrieval System (CESARS), 98
Chemical Exposure, 41
Chemical Industry Notes, 131
Chemical Reactions Documentation Service (CRDS), 98
Chemical Regulations and Guidelines System (CRGS), 161
Chemicals Identified in Feral and Food Animals, 41
Chemicals Identified in Human Biological Media, 41
Chemical Synonyms and Trade Names, 90
Chemisches Zentralblatt, 98
CHEMLAW, 161
CHEMLINE, 30, 91
CHEMNAME, 41
CHEMSEARCH, 42
CHEMSIS, 30, 42, 91
CHEMZERO, 42
Child Abuse and Neglect, 66
CLAIMS/CITATION, 98
CLAIMS/CLASS, 99
CLAIMS/COMPOUND REGISTRY, 99
CLAIMS/UNITERM, 99
CLAIMS/U.S. PATENT ABSTRACTS, 99
Clinical Toxicology of Commercial Products (CTCP), 42
Code of Federal Regulations, 161, 162, 163
COFFEELINE, 42
COLD REGIONS, 99
Commerce Business Daily, 131
COMPENDEX, 94, 100, 102
Comprehensive Dissertation Index, 43, 66, 100, 132, 150
Computer and Information Systems Abstracts, 102
Computers and Control Abstracts, 87, 93, 105
Computer tag, 165
Conference Papers Index, 100
Congressional Information Service, 67
Congressional Record Abstracts, 69
Connect time, 165
Corpus Juris Secundum, 60, 159
COSATI codes, 62, 93, 128

CRDS. *See* Chemical Reactions Documentation Service
CRECORD, 67
CRGS. *See* Chemical Regulation and Guidelines System
Criminal Justice Periodicals Index, 67
CRIS. *See* Current Research Information System
CRT, 166
CRYST. *See* X-Ray Crystallography Search System
Crystal Data Determinative Tables, 112
CTCP. *See* Clinical Toxicology of Commercial Products
Current Index to Journals in Education, 56
Current Research Information System (CRIS), 43, 49

Database, 166
Database producer, 166
Data communications network, 166
DEADLINE DATA ON WORLD AFFAIRS, 67
Descriptive Word Index, 160
Descriptor, 166
DIALOG, 3, 125, 156
Digest of Research in the Electric Utility Industry, 102
DISC, 101
DISCLOSURE II, 132
Dissertation Abstracts International, 43, 66, 100, 132, 150
DOE Energy Data Base, 63, 73, 92, 101
DOW JONES NEWS, 132
Downloading, 167
DRUGINFO, 43
Drug Research Reports (*The Blue Sheet*), 48
Duns Market Identifiers, 133

EBIB. *See* Energy Bibliography and Index
Economics Abstracts International, 68
Economic Titles/Abstracts, 68
EI Engineering Meetings (EIMET), 102
Eighteenth Century Short Title Catalog (ESTC), 150
EIMET. *See* EI Engineering Meetings
EIS: Environmental Impact Statements, 44
EIS Industrial Plants, 133
EIS Nonmanufacturing Establishments, 134
ELCOM. *See* Electronics and Computers
Electrical and Electronics Abstracts, 87, 93, 105
Electric Power Database, 102
Electric Power Industry Abstracts, 102
Electronic Legislative Search System (ELSS), 161
Electronics and Communications Abstracts, 102
Electronics and Computers (ELCOM), 102
Electronic Yellow Pages, 133
ELSS. *See* Electronic Legislative Search System
Encyclopedia of Economics, 60
Encyclopedia of World Art, 148
End user, 167
Energy Bibliography and Index (EBIB), 101
Energy Data Base Subject Thesaurus, 91, 94, 102
Energy Information Abstracts, 103
ENERGYLINE, 103
ENERGYNET, 103
Energy Research Abstracts, 101
Engineering Index, 94, 100
ENVIROLINE, 44, 102
Environment Abstracts, 103
Environmental Bibliography, 44, 103

Environmental Periodicals Bibliography, 104
Enzyme Commission numbers, 30
Enzyme Nomenclature, 30
Epilepsy Abstracts, 44
EPILEPSYLINE, 44
ERIC, 55, 57, 68
ESTC. *See* Eighteenth Century Short Title Catalog
Exceptional Child Education Resources, 59, 68
Excerpta Medica, 45

Fair Employment Practices Cases, 162
False hit, 167
Family Resources Database, 69
FDC Reports (The Pink Sheet), 48
Federal Energy Data Index (FEDEX), 69
Federal Register Search System (FRSS), 162
Federal Reporter, 156, 158, 159
Federal Supplement, 164
FEDEX. *See* Federal Energy Data Index
FIND/SVP Reports and Studies Index, 134
Fine Chemicals Directory, 104
FINTEL Newsbase, 134
FOODS ADLIBRA, 45
Food Science and Technology Abstracts, 45
Foreign Traders Index (FTI), 134
Forest Products, 46
Free text, 167
Frost & Sullivan, 134
FRSS. *See* Federal Register Search System
FTI. *See* Foreign Traders Index
Full text, 167

Genetics Abstracts, 46
GEOARCHIVE, 104
GEOCOM Bulletin, 104
Geomechanics Abstracts (GMA), 104
GEOREF, 104
GEOREF Thesaurus and Guide to Indexing, 95, 105
GEOTITLES Weekly, 104
Glossary of ASTM Definitions, 91
GMA. *See* Geomechanics Abstracts
Government Reports Announcements and Index, 62, 109, 128
GPO Monthly Catalog, 69

HARFAX Industry Data Sources, 135
Harvard Business Review, 135
Health Planning and Administration, 46
Herbage Abstracts, 23
Highway Safety Literature Abstracts, 114
HISTLINE, 70
Historical Abstracts, 70
History, 142
Hospital Literature Index, 46
HOT SPECS, 108
How to Name an Organic Substance, 89
Humanities Index, 146

Identifier, 168
IEEE Standard Dictionary of Electrical and Electronic Terms, 91
Index, coordinate, 9, 11–13, 19, 165
Index, hierarchical, 8–9
Index of Economic Articles, 70
Index Medicus, 25, 30, 50
Index to the American Banker, 130
Index to Publications of the United States Congress, 67
Information Bank Thesaurus and User Guide, 74
Information utility, 168
INPADOC, 105
INPADOC Patent Gazette, 105
INSPEC, 38, 87, 105
INSPEC Thesaurus, 93, 105

Instructional Resources Information System (IRIS), 70
Insurance Abstracts, 135
International Bibliography (*MLA*), 143, 151
International Encyclopedia of the Social Sciences, 60
International Labour Documentation, 135
International Minicomputer Software Directory, 105
International Pharmaceutical Abstracts, 46
International Software Database, 105
Introduction to Chemical Nomenclature, 89
Inverted index, 168
IRIS. *See* Instructional Resources Information System
IRL Life Science Collection, 46
ISI/BIOMED, 47
ISI/COMPUMATH, 106
ISI/Index to Scientific & Technical Proceedings & Books, 106
ISMEC, 106
ISMEC Bulletin, 106

Journal of Economic Literature, 70
Journal of Synthetic Methods, 98
Journal of the Society of Architectural Historians (JSAH), 150
JSAH. *See* Journal of the Society of Architectural Historians

Key to Economic Science and Management Science, 68
Keyword, 168
KWIC (Keyword in context), 9–10
KWOC (Keyword out of context), 9–10

Labor Arbitration Reports, 162
LABORDOC, 135
LABORLAW, 162
Labor Relations Reporter, 162
Language and Language Behavior Abstracts (LLBA), 151
Language of Twentieth Century Music, The (Fink and Ricci), 147
LC/LINE, 71, 147, 151
LC/MARC, 71, 151
Legal Periodicals Index, 155
Legal Resource Index, 75, 158, 162
Legal Thesaurus, 160
LEXIS, 159, 162
Library and Information Science Abstracts (LISA), 71
Library of Congress Subject Headings, 60, 71, 147
Library of Congress Subject Headings for Recordings of Western Non-Classical Music, 148
Life Insurance Abstracts, 135
LISA. *See* Library and Information Science Abstracts
LLBA. *See* Language and Language Behavior Abstracts
Lundberg Letter, 137

Machine Readable Cataloging (MARC), 71, 151
Magazine Index, 71
Malimet, 45
Management and Marketing Abstracts (MMA), 136
Management Contents, 75, 136, 139
Management Contents Data Base Thesaurus, 125
MARC. *See* Machine Readable Cataloging
Mass Spectral Search System, 107
Mass Spectrometry Bulletin, 107
Master List of Medical Terms. See Malimet
Mathematical Reviews, 87, 107
MATHFILE, 87, 107

Medical Subject Headings (MeSH), 31, 34
Medical Subject Headings—Supplementary Chemical Records, 1983, 30
MEDLARS, 3
MEDLINE, 15, 25, 46, 47
Mental Health Abstracts, 72
Merck Index, 29, 31, 90
MeSH. See Medical Subject Headings
METADEX. *See* Metals Abstracts and Alloys Index
Metals Abstracts and Alloys Index (METADEX), 108
Metals Abstracts, 94, 108
Meteorological and Geoastrophysical Abstracts, 108
Microbiology Abstracts, 23, 46
Microcomputer Index, 108
Microcomputer Software Directory, 105
Middle East Economic Survey, 137
Military & Federal Specifications and Standards, 108
Military Specifications and Services, 108
Military Standard Drawings, 108
Million Dollar Directory, 136
Mine Safety and Health Cases, 162
MMA. *See* Management and Marketing Abstracts
Modem, 168
Modern Language Association Bibliography. *See* International Bibliography (MLA)
Monitor, 72
Monthly Catalog of the National Agricultural Library, 39

National Criminal Justice Reference Service (NCJRS), 72
National Information Center for Educational Media Index, 75
National Information Sources on the Handicapped, 73
National Newspaper Index, 72, 75
National Rehabilitation Information Center (NRIC), 73
National Technical Information Service (NTIS), 47, 62, 73, 93, 109, 158
NCJRS. *See* National Criminal Justice Reference Service
New Grove Dictionary of Music and Musicians, The (Sadie, ed.), 148
NEWSEARCH, 74–75, 138
Newspaper Index, 74
New York Times Information Bank, 74
New York Times Online, 74
NEXIS, 136, 137
NICEM, 75
NICSEM/NIMIS, 75
NMRLIT, 109
Nomenclature of Organic Chemistry, 89
Nonferrous Metals Abstracts, 109
NRIC. *See* National Rehabilitation Information Center
NTIS. *See* National Technical Information Service

Occupational Safety and Health Cases, 162
Oceanic Abstracts, 48
Official Gazette of the U.S. Patent Office, 99
Offline, 169
OHM-TADS. *See* Oil and Hazardous Materials–Technical Assistance Data System
Oil and Hazardous Materials–Technical Assistance Data System (OHM-TADS), 110
Online, 169
Online vendor, 169
ORBIT, 3, 156

PAIS Foreign Language Index, 75
PAIS International, 75
PAPERCHEM, 110
PATLAW, 163

PATSEARCH, 110
P/E NEWS, 137
Pharmaceutical News Index, 48
Philosopher's Index, 147
Philosopher's Index Thesaurus, 147
Physics Abstracts, 87, 93, 105
PIRA Abstracts, 110
Platt's Oilgram News Service, 137
Political Science Thesaurus II, 57, 59, 80, 126
Pollution Abstracts, 111
POPLINE, 76
Popline Thesaurus, 76
Power, 111
Population Bibliography, 76
Predicasts Source Index, 138
Predicasts Terminal System Reference Manual, 125, 128
Property and Liability Index, 135
PSYCHINFO, 120, 126
Psychological Abstracts, 61, 76
Psychopharmacology Abstracts, 72
PTS Annual Reports Abstracts, 132, 137
PTS F&S Indexes, 125, 137
PTS International Forecasts, 76
PTS International Time Series, 77
PTS PROMT, 138
PTS U.S. Forecasts, 77
PTS U.S. Time Series, 77
Public Affairs Information Service Bulletin, 60, 75, 155

QUEBEC, 77

RAPRA. *See* Rubber and Plastics Research Abstracts
Registry of Toxic Effects of Chemical Substances (RTECS), 48
REMARC, 147
Resources in Computer Education (RICE), 78
Resources in Education, 56
Resources in Vocational Education (RIVE), 59, 64, 78
Review of Metal Literature, 108
Reviews of Applied Entomology, 23, 41
RICE. *See* Resources in Computer Education
RILM (Répertoire International de Littérature Musicale) Abstracts, 152
RIVE. *See* Resources in Vocational Education
RTECS. *See* Registry of Toxic Effects of Chemical Substances
Rubber and Plastics Research Abstracts (RAPRA), 111

SAE Abstracts, 111
Safety, 112
Safety Science Abstracts Journal, 112
SANSS. *See* Structure and Nomenclature Searching System
Science Abstracts, 105
Science Citation Index, 23
SCISEARCH, 25, 49, 106
Searchable Physics Information Notes (SPIN), 112
Search profile construction, 19–20
Selected Water Resources Abstracts, 50
Shepard's Citations, 163
SHE: Subject Headings for Engineering, 94
SIC. *See* Standard Industrial Classification Codes
Single Crystal Reduction and Search System (XTAL), 112
Social Sciences Citation Index, 12, 125, 158
Social SCISEARCH (SSCI), 78
Sociological Abstracts, 57, 60
Sociological Abstracts, xiii, 62, 129
SPIN. *See* Searchable Physics Information Notes
Sport, 79
Sport and Recreation Index, 79
SSCI. *See* Social SCISEARCH
SSIE Current Research, 43, 49
Standard & Poor's News, 138

Standard Industrial Classification Manual, 127
Standard Industrial Classification Codes (SIC), 125, 126, 127
Standards & Specifications, 112, 113
Structure & Nomenclature Searching System (SANSS), 113
Superindex, 49, 113
Supreme Court Digest, 160
Supreme Court Reporter, 156, 164
Surface Coating Abstracts, 113, 114
Synopsis and Classification of Living Organisms, 33

TELEGEN, 50
TELEGEN Reports, 50
Textile Technology Digest, 114
THERMO, 114
Thesaurus of Engineering and Scientific Terms, 48, 59, 73, 93, 109
Thesaurus of ERIC Descriptors, 55, 57, 59, 64, 68–69, 78, 159
Thesaurus of Marriage and Family, 69
Thesaurus of Metallurgical Terms, 94
Thesaurus of Psychological Index Terms, 59, 62, 76, 126
Thesaurus of Water Resources Terms, 48, 51, 116
Toxic Substances Control Act Chemical Substance Inventory, 29, 90
TOXLINE, 46, 50
Trade and Industry Index, 75, 138
Trade Opportunities, 139
Transportation Research Information Service (TRIS), 114
TRIS. *See* Transportation Research Information Service
TROPAG, 50
TULSA, 115

Unified Numbering System for Metals and Alloys, 88
United States Patent Law Quarterly, 163
UPI News, 80
USCLASS, 115
U.S. Exports, 139
U.S. Patent Alerts, 115
U.S. Political Science Documentation, 59, 79, 125
U.S. Public School Directory, 80

Veterinary Bulletin, 41

Wage and Hours Cases, 162
WATERDROP, 115–116
WATERNET, 116
Water Resources Abstracts, 50–51, 116
Weed Abstracts, 41
WELDASEARCH, 116
WESTLAW, 15, 155–156, 158, 160, 164
West's Federal Practice Digest, 2d, 154, 160
Wiswesser Line Notation, 48, 104
Words and Phrases, 160
Words That Mean Business, 124
World Affairs Report, 80
World Aluminum Abstracts, 117
Worldcasts Basebook, 77
Worldcasts Composites, 77
World Textiles, 51, 117
World Textiles Abstracts, 117

X-Ray Crystallography Search System (CRYST), 117
XTAL. *See* Single Crystal Reduction and Search System

Zinc, Lead, and Cadmium Abstracts, 117–118
Zoological Record, xiii, 51
Zoological Record, 6, 51

For Product Safety Concerns and Information please contact our EU representative GPSR@taylorandfrancis.com Taylor & Francis Verlag GmbH, Kaufingerstraße 24, 80331 München, Germany

Batch number: 10725889

Printed by Printforce, the Netherlands